How to Make a Life

How to Make a Life

A Tibetan Refugee Family and the
Midwestern Woman They Adopted

Madeline Uraneck

WISCONSIN HISTORICAL SOCIETY PRESS

Published by the Wisconsin Historical Society Press
Publishers since 1855

The Wisconsin Historical Society helps people connect to the past by
collecting, preserving, and sharing stories. Founded in 1846, the Society
is one of the nation's finest historical institutions.
Join the Wisconsin Historical Society: wisconsinhistory.org/membership

A portion of the sales of this book will be donated to the Wisconsin
Tibetan Association.

For permission to reuse material from *How to Make a Life*
(ISBN 978-0-87020-855-3; e-book ISBN 978-0-87020-856-0),
please access www.copyright.com or contact the Copyright
Clearance Center, Inc. (CCC), 222 Rosewood Drive, Danvers, MA 01923, 978-
750-8400. CCC is a not-for-profit organization that
provides licenses and registration for a variety of users.

Images are by Madeline Uraneck unless otherwise noted.
The back cover image by Peter Williams shows Migmar and Tenzin
in traditional Tibetan dress.

Printed in the United States of America
Designed by Integrated Composition Systems

22 21 20 19 18   1 2 3 4 5

Library of Congress Cataloging-in-Publication Data

Names: Uraneck, Madeline, author.
Title: How to make a life : a Tibetan refugee family and the Midwestern woman
they adopted / Madeline Uraneck.
Other titles: Tibetan refugee family and the Midwestern woman they adopted
Description: Madison, WI : Wisconsin Historical Society Press, [2018] |
Identifiers: LCCN 2018002467 (print) | LCCN 2018003203 (ebook) |
ISBN 9780870208560 (ebook) | ISBN 9780870208553 (pbk. : alk. paper)
Subjects: LCSH: Uraneck, Madeline. | Tibetans—Wisconsin—Madison—
Biography. | Tenzin Kalsang, 1962– | Tibetan-Americans—Social life and
customs. | Women immigrants—Wisconsin—Madison—Biography. | Single
women—Wisconsin—Madison—Biography. | Single women—Family
relationships—Wisconsin—Madison. | Refugees—United States—Biography.
| Immigrants—Family relationships—Wisconsin—Madison.
Classification: LCC F589.M19 (ebook) | LCC F589.M19 T53 2018 (print) |
DDC 305.895/41073—dc23
LC record available at https://lccn.loc.gov/2018002467

To the memory of my parents, Carl and Barbara Uraneck,
who hinted for a story or a poem as a gift for their every birthday,
Mother's Day, Father's Day, and Christmas of my childhood,

to my country school teacher, Dale R. Jordan,
who inspired detailed outlines, multiple drafts,
diagrammed sentences,
and responses to five decades of personal letters,

and to Tenzin Kalsang, who smiled when she said, "Tibet!"

Contents

Author's Note

As I collected the stories shared here, my written notes became repetitive swirls of Tenzins, Pemas, and Migmars—names that are commonly repeated in Tibetan culture, often within households. The first name Tenzin is especially common because it means someone has been named by the Fourteenth Dalai Lama (see page 10 for a more detailed explanation of this process). Most Tibetans have both a first and a second name, with profound, lovely, or religious meanings, but rarely a common last name for the family as is conventional in many other cultures.

Among close family members and friends, a person might be called by just one of their given names—either the first or second, or by a word that indicates their family relation, such as *ani* (older sister) or *chungpo* (younger brother). For example, in the family I came to know, Tenzin Kalsang is called *ama-lak* (mother) by her children and Tenzin Kalsang by her husband. Her sons, Tenzin Tamdin and Tenzin Thardoe, are usually called simply Tamdin and Thardoe. But when visiting larger groups of family or friends, with many names overlapping, people might use one another's full names, nicknames, or titles (such as *genlak* for teacher) to avoid confusion and to indicate respect or affection. Away from the pages of this book, in my interactions with them, I often use their double names, or one name followed by "-lak," to make clear my respect. When everyone calls a favorite uncle *acho* (older brother), however, I find myself doing the same.

For the purposes of this text, I refer to the main members of the family by just one of their given names after giving their full name on first reference, to minimize confusion as much as possible. For some members of the extended family and others who are in the book on a more limited basis, I have used just one of their given names throughout, to help preserve the anonymity of those who did not choose to be written about. Below is a list of recurring names, which should be referred to as needed for reference. Besides trying to balance respect, anonymity, and simplicity, I erred on the side of caution when a few individuals who appear in the book on a limited basis asked that I not use their full or real names at all. Given the nature of their or their relatives' political activities in diaspora communities or in the Tibetan Autonomous Region of China, I honored these requests. In these few cases, we agreed upon an alternate name to be used.

Tenzin Kalsang (Tenzin), wife of Migmar Dorjee
Migmar Dorjee (Migmar), husband of Tenzin Kalsang
Namgyal Tsedup (Namgyal), Tenzin and Migmar's
    eldest son
Nawang Lhadon (Lhadon), Tenzin and Migmar's
    daughter
Tenzin Tamdin (Tamdin), Tenzin and Migmar's second
    son
Tenzin Thardoe (Thardoe), Tenzin and Migmar's
    youngest son
Pema Choedon, Tenzin's mother
Tsewang Paldon, Tenzin's father
Dickey Norzom (Dickey), Tenzin's younger sister
Damdul, Dickey's husband in Delhi, India
Migkyi, Migmar's sister who was left behind in Tibet
Tseten Lhamo (Acha Lhamo), Tenzin and Dickey's older
    half-sister
Pema Khando (Khando-lak), Lhamo's husband

Tsamchoe, Thardoe's host mother in Dharamsala, India

Migmar Wangdu (Wangdu), Thardoe's host father in
  Dharamsala

Lhakpa, Namgyal's wife, from Dharamsala

Namdol, Lhakpa's older sister in Dharamsala

Samkyi, Thardoe's wife, from Bylakuppe, India

Tenzin Choesang (Choesang), daughter of Lhakpa and
  Namgyal, first grandchild of Migmar and Tenzin

Tseten, Tamdin's girlfriend

Jampa Khedup, elder brother of Thardoe's wife Samkyi

Tenzin Dechen (Dechen), Lhadon's husband, from Nepal

Gawa (Acho Gawa), Migmar's nephew, Bylakuppe, India

Choenzom (Ani Choenzom), wife of Gawa, Bylakuppe

CHAPTER 1

Stumbling into a Family

*Birds fly above and around us every hour of every day, and
we barely notice them. But if one flies crookedly, it captures
our attention. Those things which are outwardly peculiar
are most liable to stimulate our sense, so that we seek the
inner meaning.*
  —JALAL AL-DIN AL-RUMI, THIRTEENTH-CENTURY
  SUFI POET, AFGHANISTAN AND ASIATIC TURKEY

If those who journey abroad are categorized as either tourists,
travelers, or global citizens, I fall somewhere between traveler
and global citizen. I've taught English in Japan and researched
globalization in Morocco. I've studied dance in Sweden and
Poland, worked for the Peace Corps in Central Asia, and have
been a Peace Corps volunteer in southern Africa. Whether
through work, study, or adventures, I have passed through
sixty-four countries. But the most important journey I've ever
taken was one I hadn't even realized I had been on. It began in
1994—without an airline ticket, vaccinations, or an itinerary—
in Madison, Wisconsin.

One afternoon, a smiling dark-haired woman came to dust
my office cubicle files. In the manner of a friendly midwest-
erner, I said hello and asked her name and where she was from.

Since that day, Tenzin Kalsang has led me to places I never could have traveled on my own. Improbably and over time, we became family.

Born in a refugee settlement in India to Tibetan parents, Tenzin had arrived in the United States in 1993. We met before her teenage children and husband came to join her. When they finally did, on a family reunification visa, I acted as their guide. In turn, their family taught me profound lessons about hope, human rights, and cultural change.

I'm still not sure why I never had children of my own. I'm an educator who's worked in dozens of schools in Wisconsin and around the world, and I've long delighted in spending time with kids. I joke that when I travel, I have family radar. On a bus or in a shop while roving overseas, I catch the eye of a curious child and ask her name. Soon the mother comes to take the hand of her child, and in my halting Swedish or Japanese or Sesotho, I tell them where I am from. I have a knack for wrangling an invitation into homes, where tea or dinner or maybe even an overnight may follow. These families often have multiple children, just as my Oklahoma family included five sisters and brothers. Unlike my own stepmother, the matrons in these families might be large and buxom, delighted to watch their children interact with an international wayfarer. These encounters spoke to my mothering needs and healed a broken part of me. I had always yearned for a family of my own. I wanted to be part of a holistic, chaotic human bundle.

I became part of my Tibetan American family slowly—at first befriending just Tenzin Kalsang, then, four years later, her husband and children. In some ways, entering their house was like crossing a border into a foreign country. They introduced me to their colorful holidays, their wholesome foods, their religious practices, and the different ways they raised their children. Like immigrants before them, they deftly and necessarily blended, changed, and melded old with new. Over time, when the children began bypassing chances to listen to their father's stories or learn about their history and their written language, when they started shortening holidays and skipping religious services, I wanted to shout, "No! Keep these precious things." The loss felt familiar.

In 1920, my own grandparents left one mining town on the Czech-Polish border for another mining town in northern Michigan. I never witnessed their struggles. My grandmother, who spoke only Polish, died in the 1930s before I was born. My father seldom mentioned that he had been raised in a family that spoke another language. The material remnants of my Polish heritage were one wedding photo, four crocheted doilies, a recipe for latkes, and my grandmother's traditional dress from Cieszyn. My grandmother never got a chance to show me how to pickle mushrooms or paint *pisanky* Easter eggs. My grandfather never explained to me why they had left—I can imagine stories of poverty, military induction, and ethnic strife. By the time I was curious, they were both gone.

I would not have despaired the loss of my grandparents' cultural heritage, or perhaps even gotten as involved with Tenzin's family, had I not found Folklore Village, a rural folk arts center forty miles west of Madison, with large gardens, two bunkhouses, and a one-room schoolhouse. It was the legacy of its quirky founder, Jane Farwell. Folklore Village introduced visitors to world music, dances, crafts, foods, and folklore, and I reveled in my minimally paid work there on and off during two decades in my twenties and thirties. Even though its view of folklore and immigrant traditions was often romantic and Eurocentric, it was through Folklore Village that I came to understand how much we Americans have lost by being ignorant or dismissive of our own immigrant past.

But the re-creations of ethnic celebrations at Folklore Village had a make-believe aspect to them. When I met Tenzin's family, I experienced holidays in context and customs in daily practice, changing almost imperceptibly from one year to the next. What Tenzin's family had, what I saw disassembling before my eyes, seemed the very thing I had been seeking—intergenerational families, profound beliefs, old stories and songs, intricate dance steps, and customs that could connect me to a vibrant heritage of meaning.

At the heart of this journey is one of America's oldest stories, the story of its immigrants. When I started writing it, however, I discovered what new writers often find, that literary paths rarely stray far from one's own fences. My own journey—that I lost a mother when I was very young; that I was a bossy eldest child who mothered four siblings; that I am a single, divorced woman with no children—crisscrosses Tenzin's and her family's. They were a family who needed to adjust; I was a single person who needed the wholesome connections that a close-knit family could offer. They bumped against the contradictions of US public schools head-on, enabling me to see how the very policies I implemented in my work for the state education department had little trickle-down in classrooms. In the beginning of knowing them, I thought I had much to offer. Every year I became more humble and more touched by their gifts of strength, modesty, and willingness to share.

While writing about our intertwined paths, I have often asked myself, who am I to tell Tenzin's story? I am not Tibetan, not a refugee, not a Buddhist. I am not one of her children. The family spoke Tibetan at home, but despite my attempt to study the language, I couldn't hear the four tones in even the very first letters of its alphabet: *Ka, kha, kha, nga*. I am a white woman of middle-class privilege. They are people of color tossed onto the bottom rungs of the US economy.

So I was very nervous the evening I asked if could write a book about our years together. Migmar and Tenzin's stories seemed remarkable, and I had collected many humorous anecdotes about the family's adjustments and my misunderstandings of their culture. They seemed pleased, if curious why I would want to write about them. Over many months, they graciously answered my repeated questions, volunteered additional information, and requested I omit only a few incidents. I have fretted about my accuracy, their feelings, and how others, especially in Tibetan American communities, might judge this act of trespassing. But they seemed less concerned about how they would be portrayed and more willing to trust another to share intimate details than I would have been myself. When I tried to read sections of what I had written, they brushed me off, saying, "We know, Madeline. We told you that."

While grateful for their support and confidence, I became increasingly aware the story I was telling was as much mine as theirs. Rather than a strictly nonfiction recital of events, I was writing a memoir: reflections on our time together, my perceptions of our interactions, and the ways knowing them had changed me. In small, daily ways, this family challenged the stark angularity of my Anglo-European perspectives and helped me to understand the world in ways that were gentler, more forgiving, and more encompassing. Over many years, their story had grafted itself onto my own, and our steps journeyed past the signposts of strength, weakness, pain, and hope that are familiar along America's multicultural roads. When we say that immigrants add to America's diversity, we do not mean they remain in isolated enclaves. Their experiences blend with, meld with, and enrich the lives of those they befriend, live next door to, work with, and marry.

However they arrive, asylum seekers, immigrants, and

refugees reach with outstretched hands toward safer, more promising shores. Welcoming these wayfarers rekindles our humanity and heals our broken parts. Only within the cords that bind us together do we find answers to age-old questions about despair and enmity, fear and alienation, justice and hope.

CHAPTER 2

Tenzin's Story

*The choices we make lead up to actual experiences. It is one
thing to decide to climb a mountain. It is quite another to be
on top of it.*
—HERBERT A. SIMON, AMERICAN SOCIAL
SCIENTIST AND NOBEL PRIZE LAUREATE

The cleaning woman with the thick, dark braid changed my life.
I entered my cubicle, holding a coffee mug with its bitter, end-of-
day roast and found her dusting my file cabinets. She turned to
grin, and a silver tooth caught the glint of the fluorescent lights.

Other state employees, at their desks since the early morning hours, had left for the day, and a momentary quiet drifted
over the empty workspaces. I stayed late, hoping to finish curriculum drafts or read international updates. Elevator doors
banged open, and I heard the cleaning staff wheeling trash containers, mops, and buckets down the halls, noisily reporting for
carpet and linoleum duty.

Although my job title had the word "international" in it—
international education consultant at Wisconsin's state education department—it was in my after-hours conversations with
cleaning staff that my day sometimes assumed unexpected
global hues.

Custodial work often is among immigrants' earliest employment when they arrive in the United States, and our building's maintenance crew seemed to have ever-changing faces from Mexico, Guatemala, and India. I would often ask the newcomers, as they vacuumed the carpet or emptied the trash can beneath my desk, where they had come from, and why. "Why" is the connective tissue between an immigrant's personal story and a global issue—whether it's a civil war, an overthrown dictator, drug lord terrorism, reunion with family members, or simply hope for a better job.

"Hi, what's your name?" I asked the woman with the braid.

"Tenzin," she said. She laughed as she answered. Even in that first exchange I noticed the laugh—merriment, I wondered, or self-consciousness?

"Where are you from?" I asked.

I knew this was not always a welcome question. But she answered emphatically, with a proud smile. "Tibet!"

Tibet! I winced guiltily. One year earlier, I had attended an orientation meeting for the Tibetan Resettlement Project, a remarkable, well-organized initiative to help soon-to-arrive Tibetan refugees from India and Nepal find homes and jobs in Madison. With two other volunteers, I had been assigned the name of a newcomer. Months had passed. I should have called to find out what was happening, but I was busy, and no one had called me, either. I hoped the other two women had made contact with our assigned person.

I asked Tenzin if she had been part of Madison's original arrivals in the Tibetan Resettlement Project.

To my surprise, she said no. She had disembarked from a Greyhound bus in Madison only a few months earlier, in March 1993, all alone, a self-appointed transfer from Charlottesville, Virginia, another designated resettlement city.

"I arrived Virginia," Tenzin explained in her rudimentary

English. "Batch 14, next to last batch. My friend told me Madison better."

I wasn't familiar with "batch" but figured it was a way that arrivals were grouped. Her friend was someone she had known in India and was indeed one of Madison's original arrivals. I would later learn that in Virginia, Tenzin had worked for nine months as a live-in housekeeper for an affluent family. She worked six days a week for three hundred dollars a month, plus room and board, and sent most of her earnings back to her husband and children in India. She felt lonely and isolated. With little more than her friend's address written on a scrap of paper, plus some wages she had saved, Tenzin boarded a bus for a city nine hundred miles away. She didn't know the name of the state.

"Do you have children?" I asked her, still standing with my coffee cup.

"Four!" She laughed again.

I felt dismayed. "How young is the youngest?"

"Seven," she said, giggling.

I lost my own mother at age four. My heart ached as I imagined four faraway children whose mother was here dusting my office furniture.

"Who is taking care of them?"

"My husband," Tenzin said. She smiled reassuringly, as if I might be thinking she had left them all alone. "And grandfather."

Even in that two-minute conversation, I felt confident I could help her.

I had it wrong.

❧

Tenzin told me her story in small pieces, a sentence here, an answer to a question there. She introduced me to other Tibetan Americans whose stories were both unique and similar to her own. Take her name: Tenzin Kalsang. Just about any Tibetan knows that a man or woman named Tenzin has been personally named by His Holiness the Dalai Lama, whose name is Tenzin Gyatso. In the Tibetan language, *Tenzin* means "holder of the teachings" or "protector of the Dharma."

Most Tibetans-in-exile throughout the United States, Asia, and Europe live thousands of miles from His Holiness the Dalai Lama. For His Holiness to name a child involves a personal assembly line wherein a friend or relative, or a friend of a friend of a friend, submits a request in writing or in person in Dharamsala, India, where the Dalai Lama resides. Each child named in this way receives two names—the first is always Tenzin, after His Holiness. If the Dalai Lama himself is not present, a monk or lama draws the second name from one of two bowls of names His Holiness has selected, one for girls, the other for boys. The name might be texted or phoned back to the expecting parents, then shortly afterward, usually via a series of traveling relatives or friends of friends, arrives a yellow envelope on which is printed a prayer. The envelope contains tiny brown capsules of medicinal herbs and a blessed thread. The thread is tied around the child's neck, wrist, or chest to ward off bad dreams and evil spirits and to give the baby an auspicious start in life. Children with names other than Tenzin have similar religious connections to their names' meanings and name givers. (See page 235 for more on name meanings.)

Tenzin's second name, Kalsang, which is not a surname, means "good fortune." When speaking with her and other ethnic Tibetans, I learned to inquire after and use both given names. In Tenzin's immediate family, for example, the heads of any one of four people might pop up if I merely called out, "Tenzin?" As I had more encounters with her family and friends, I started to follow her name with "*lak*," which sounded to my ear like *lah*, to indicate affection and respect.

❦

"Madeline! You busy? I have a question."

Tenzin occasionally stopped by my cubicle at the end of my workday to ask an array of questions. She often asked about money market CDs, investments, and mortgages. Even though she had never gone beyond seventh grade in India, she had an acute knack for financial management.

After Tenzin had lived in the United States for three years and became eligible to apply for a family reunification visa, she asked me where she could rent an apartment for her family, and if I would help her fill out forms to bring them from India.

I was a lifelong renter who never borrowed money. I had no children, no CDs in the bank, and I chose my apartments for their lopsided charm without concern for neighborhood schools. I was as frustrated by the tiny font on the forms from the US Immigration and Citizenship Services as she was. Fortunately Tenzin asked the same questions of everyone she met, including other Tibetans in Madison, both the new arrivals and those long-established, and she accumulated good advice.

Working for seven dollars an hour, Tenzin soon had more money in her savings account than I did. "I sent three hundred dollars to my mom today. She's sick," she would say. Or, "I sent my sister four hundred dollars. She's going to give it to my niece, for tuition." Or, "I sent five hundred dollars for Tibet, for freedom." I looked at the carpet cleaners and trash bin collectors in my building with deepening respect.

❦

Though she called herself Tibetan, Tenzin had never been to Tibet, and she doubted she would ever have a chance to set foot there. Her mother, Pema Choedon, was born in 1919 in the

village of Tsera, in Kham, one of the three main regions of old
Tibet. Pema Choedon married a businessman and gave birth at
home to six children, with no midwife. Tenzin told me her pregnant mother would take clean cloths and a basin of water and
climb the ladder to the room where the family lived, on the floor
above the animal stables. After delivering her own baby, she
would climb down the ladder later in the day to cook and feed
the animals. Three of her children would later die of smallpox
or other infant diseases.

One day Pema's first husband was robbed and killed as he
rode his horse between villages. I wanted to know more, but
Tenzin seemed to have few details. "I wasn't born yet," she said.
To Tenzin, her mother's history resembled that of other elders.
She did not seem to find it remarkable, and I had to read and
interview other elders to understand the context of those turbulent times.

Despite the passage of time since Tenzin's mother's exodus,
the dispute over Tibet's loss of sovereignty, culture, and popu-
lace remains a thorn in the Republic of China's relations with
its ethnic peoples and the rest of the world. The history between
China and Tibet is ancient, complex, and controversial, but
China's larger, more powerful muscle, surrounding and covet-
ing the vast spaces of its resource-rich neighbor, made Tibet
easy prey. One major invasion, recorded in October 1950, began
a stormy decade that scarred the lives of Tibetans who lived
through it and the generations who followed.

After her first husband's death, Pema Choedon remarried to
a man named Tsewang Paldon. In 1959, following the Chinese
army's suppression of a bloody Tibetan uprising, the couple
joined thousands of Tibetans fleeing over the snow-covered
mountains to bordering Bhutan, Nepal, and India. Wealthy,
educated government officials and nobility struggled alongside

monks and peasants. Pema Choedon and Tsewang Paldon carried and walked with their surviving three children.

As they fled, Pema Choedon and her husband did not have
ready access to news to understand the world-spinning crisis
around them. Rumors and fact passed by word of mouth from one
refugee to another, often months after events happened. The
Chinese government erased the word "Tibet" from world maps,
renamed it Xizang Province, and barred re-entry to the estimated
eighty thousand Tibetans who had left homes, animals, families,
and friends behind. Chinese soldiers burned Tibetan Buddhist
monasteries; jailed, tortured, and killed Tibetan activists; and
targeted landowners and nobility around the religious communities whose monasteries encompassed vast land holdings.

The young Dalai Lama and his ministers had escaped to
India on a twenty-day journey, ending on April 18, 1959. As he
struggled to establish a government-in-exile, he despaired over
reports of Tibetans who followed him, falling ill or dying during
their long escape route. What does a country do, overwhelmed
by thousands of its desperate neighbors? Indian and Nepalese
emissaries pleaded emphatically at the United Nations, declaring
they could house the Tibetans only temporarily. Already poor
countries, they could not take on unspecified thousands of
impoverished people. While diplomats entreated, Tibetans continued to pour into India through snowy mountain border passes.

Historical documents reveal that most neighboring countries,
as well as the United States and the United Nations, offered few
solutions to Tibetan pleas for help. But the Dalai Lama found a
solid ally in Indian Prime Minister Jawaharlal Nehru. Nehru
worked with the Dalai Lama to quickly build Tibetan refugee
settlements throughout India, from the cool, mountainous north
to the hot, tropical south. From the beginning, both the prime
minister and His Holiness envisioned the settlements as

distinct from neighboring Indian communities and as refuges where Tibetan culture and religion could flourish. They imagined Buddhist temples built in the Tibetan architectural and spiritual style, the Tibetan language taught in schools, and the skills of traditional handicrafts passing to new generations.

The southern state of Karnataka, with vast tracts of undeveloped jungle, was among the first to step forward with an offer to host three thousand Tibetan settlers. Pema Choedon and Tsewang Paldon had already survived the journey from Tibet to its mountainous border, from the border to Dharamsala, and from Dharamsala to various work camps, where refugees were assigned to construct their own quarters and build roads. Sometime in 1961, along with hundreds of others, they volunteered to become pioneers and boarded one of the crowded trains that chugged slowly to Karnataka's overgrown forests.

The community that developed there, called Lugsung Samdupling Tibetan Settlement, began as seven closely spaced villages amidst the tangled jungle. Located near what is today the city of Bylakuppe, in Karnataka's Mysore District, Lugsung Samdupling and the settlements that followed were created as ambitious cooperative projects by the government of India and what at that time was called the Tibetan government-in-exile. The settlements evolved into one of the world's largest and arguably most successful refugee experiments. Years later, Austrian anthropologist Christoph von Fürer-Heimendorf called India's settlements, which grew from several to nearly four dozen, "one of the miracles of the twentieth century."

Cataclysmic events take a toll on ordinary people, however, and Pema Choedon and Tsewang Paldon were exhausted by the rapid succession of their multiple journeys. At the age of forty-three, just months after arriving in southern India, Pema Choedon gave birth to her seventh child, one of the first babies born in the new settlement, a daughter named Tenzin Kalsang. Pema

Choedon was fifty when she gave birth to yet another daughter, named Dickey, a Tibetan name that means "one who is happy and healthy." Pema Choedon carried Tenzin and later Dickey on her back, bound in thin cotton sheets tied with age-old knots, as she worked in the settlement's cooperatively managed fields. Shortly after Dickey's birth, Tsewang Paldon began ailing from a combination of alcoholism and severe back and body pains. Pema Choedon feared it might be polio. Whatever the diagnosis, it meant he could help little with the arduous work of caring for the farm and family in the settlement.

In the beginning, Lugsung Samdupling Tibetan Settlement consisted of one hundred households, the structures built by the refugees themselves. Although families hoped their new homes would be temporary, they worked hard to establish order. Leaders, each called a *chupon*, represented twenty-five families, and distributed information and resolved disputes among neighbors or with Indian farmers in surrounding fields. The four *chuponor* in the settlement reported to two elected *chimie*, who in turn worked with assigned representatives from the Central Tibetan Authority (CTA), with its headquarters established in northern Dharamsala.

The well-coordinated organization at Lugsung Samdupling was duplicated in other Tibetan settlements, often called camps. Growing a settlement and protecting a legacy were complex undertakings. Depending on whom you asked, shaping a settlement into a coherent cultural protectorate was an enlightened vision, an impossible dream, or an idea to be opposed. Conflicts often arose, involving a melee that might include concerned United Nations officials, nongovernmental organizations from a variety of countries, Tibetan administrators representing the CTA, local monks, and Indian villagers and farmers in the surrounding lands. The Indian government and Tibetan settlement officials did not want newly arriving Tibetan refugees to appear favored over India's other refugees, minority groups, and impoverished citizens. Most Tibetans, with their nomadic, subsistence background, were ill-prepared for the agriculture practices that were suddenly imposed on the cooperatives. Both Tibetan refugee and Indian government records reveal that during the early years of the camps, many crops and village industries were failures.

Pema Choedon's family now consisted of seven people: she and her husband, the two younger sisters born in the settlement, and the three older children who had survived the escape from Tibet. The family was allotted a one-room house and two and a half hectares (six acres) of land to farm. This was much less land than Pema Choedon and her first husband had owned in Tibet. The new land was not theirs; instead, the state of Karnataka retained ownership of the settlement land and buildings. Like most of their neighbors, neither Pema Choedon nor her husband applied to become Indian citizens in those early years. As refugees, they were not allowed to own land, vote, carry an Indian passport, or apply for local or national Indian employment. As they renewed their registration certificates each year, they nurtured a fervent hope to return to their homeland.

As a child, Tenzin attended the school in Old Camp 1, as the settlement came to be called. Like most girls in the settlement at the time, she dropped out after seventh grade. Strong and young, Tenzin was able to help her mother care for her bedridden father and work in the cooperative's cornfields.

"I didn't really even know my mother," Tenzin told me. "She was indoors, and I was outdoors."

Throughout her teenage years, Tenzin wove carpets in the central cooperative's carpet shop during the winter months and joined other women to spread manure on the fields each spring. She planted corn, using one foot and then the other to kick dirt over kernels as she walked in oxen-dug furrows. Twice a day she cut hay with a sickle, threw it into the bamboo basket that she strapped to her back, and carried it to feed the family's ten cows. Tenzin milked the cows, shopped in the market, and washed clothes in the river. At 5 p.m. every day, the water in the camp cistern was turned on, and she lined up with other women, joking and catching up with gossip, while waiting her turn with two ten-gallon aluminum pails, hung from a yoke balanced on her shoulders. The sun would be setting as she finally started for home, and I could imagine the smell of onions, garlic, and curries that beckoned as she hurried back for the second trip for water. Children played outside in the evenings, and women sat in front of their homes and sang songs, drank tea, or listened to stories. Men gathered to play cards or dice games. The days had their own pleasant rhythms.

~

Just in back of Tenzin's family's home stood an identical white cement house. Three older men lived there, all brothers. The youngest brother, Migmar Dorjee, was already in his thirties. He was a handsome soldier in the Indo-Tibetan forces and came home on leave now and then. Years later in Wisconsin, in Tenzin's intermediate English and Migmar's Tibetan, they would tell me the story of their courtship, interrupted by their grown children's gleeful translations. Tenzin and Migmar would grin and blush, as if the events had transpired only yesterday.

Pema Choedon spoke with the brothers every day, since their cow sheds were just on the other side of the bamboo fence that divided them, and she came to know Migmar's family well. When Tenzin was sixteen, Pema Choedon told her daughter, "You should be married."

"So the next time Migmar came home," Tenzin told me, "I took a close look. I told my mom, 'No, he's too old.' But she told me I had no choice."

"If you marry a man your same age," Pema Choedon told Tenzin, "then he can't do a good job of taking care of the family. You need someone who can take care of you. Migmar's age doesn't matter."

At first, Tenzin ignored her mother's advice. "But Migmar started coming over to visit when he was home on leave," Tenzin said. "He liked my mother's *chang* [rice wine], and he loved my mother. My dad agreed with me—Migmar was too old— but my mom was the power in that house."

One morning in February, Migmar stopped by with his bicycle. He had gotten permission from Tenzin's parents to take her to the Butter Lamp Festival, called Chonga Choepa, on the fifteenth and final day of the Tibetan New Year celebration. "Mother never let me go out alone, or even with the other girls," Tenzin told me. "She knew that if I got pregnant, no one would marry me. But she trusted Migmar."

Tenzin sat sideways on the back of Migmar's bike and off they went, joined by five or six other couples. The men were pedaling and the women were dressed in their finest *chupa* (traditional dresses) and striped *pangden*, or aprons, laughing and shouting to one another.

They rode to the monasteries that by then bordered the settlement and leaned their bikes against the surrounding walls. One after another, they visited the temples within the monastery grounds: Sakya Gompa, Namdroling, and Sera, each representing different Buddhist lineages. Buddhists from all over the world were sending generous donations, and residents of the nearby Tibetan settlements had contributed additional funds and labor to build these structures, at first modest but becoming more opulent with each passing year. Tenzin, Migmar, and their friends bought candles of remembrance and prayed and ate *momo*—meat-stuffed dumplings—from the food carts. The crowd swelled to thousands of people, Tibetan and Indian alike.

By early evening, they walked their bicycles through the surge of taxis, cars, and mopeds that had arrived at Tashi Lhunpo Monastery in time to watch the sunset in the monastery's courtyard. The courtyard must have been a stunning sight. It was filled with ornately carved, hand-painted yak butter sculptures of all heights, each denoting ancient Buddhist images, and thousands of flickering candles. Children sat on their fathers' shoulders, and onlookers scrambled to find good places from which to watch the music ensembles and evening's dance competition in the ethereal combination of waning sunlight, rising moonlight, and candlelight.

"Want to dance?" Migmar asked Tenzin, beckoning her to join him.

Tenzin laughed. "Oh, no," she said. "I can't dance."

Migmar grinned but went off to join the dozens of dancers. From sunset until almost 2 a.m., he danced with other young men and women from neighboring camps. Two large groups vied with one another, each one ready with a new dance the minute the other group had finished.

Judges awarded prizes to the group that had outstomped, out-twirled, and outlasted the other, and the crowds finally thinned. "Our camp won every year," Migmar told me proudly.

Far after midnight, Tenzin and Migmar returned to Old Camp 1 with their friends. I pictured them cycling home through gray shadows and the silver light of the moon.

Several days later, Migmar asked Tenzin, "Do you like me?"

Tenzin looked down at her feet, shyly laughing and blushing.

This was enough for Migmar. He cut through the backyards and strode into her house to talk with her parents. Doors throughout the settlement were unlocked, and friends and neighbors stopped in with little to-do.

"He wanted to marry me," Tenzin said, "but my father told him I was too young." Her parents explained to him when she was old enough, they would need a bridegroom who was willing to move into their home, care for them when they became old, and become head of their household.

Migmar, a youngest son, had that freedom, since his oldest brother had long been household head in that family. Still enlisted, Migmar returned to his military post in central India, biding his time. After all, he had the best ally a man could hope for—his sweetheart's mother.

Three years went by. Migmar returned home each New Year. And Pema Choedon kept up the pressure. "He comes from an honorable family in Tibet," she told her daughter. "He won't be a wife beater or a drunkard. Other men, who knows?"

Tenzin turned nineteen and finally agreed to marry Migmar. "I'm old enough now, I thought, and I was tired of her nagging."

That New Year holiday, when Migmar was again home on leave, Tenzin's mother walked through their backyards to Migmar's home.

"My daughter wants to marry your brother," Pema Choedon announced to Migmar's oldest brother. Her husband had become increasingly ill, so she insisted, in accordance with customs of Tibetan Buddhism, that there be no wedding or festivities. Thus came about the simplest of unions: the next day Migmar walked out his back door, past the sheds, through the gate, and into the open door of Tenzin's parents' home to become Tenzin's husband.

Tenzin and her aging mother had hoped the marriage would signal a greater change in their lives. But Migmar was still a soldier and had to travel back and forth between the small house in Old Camp 1 in Bylakuppe and his military assignments in central India and on the Pakistani border. The two women struggled with the farm, worked at the cooperative, and cared for Tenzin's ailing father.

Soon they had additional work. Tenzin was pregnant. "I had

baby sickness and threw up all the time. Migmar knew nothing about it." On February 28, 1982, Tenzin gave birth to their first child, a son they named Namgyal Tsedup. When the baby was two or three months old, Tenzin traveled with him to the military base to introduce Migmar to his son.

Soon she found herself pregnant again. Their daughter, Nawang Lhadon, was born in 1983 in a family unit on the military base, and their second son, Tenzin Tamdin, was born in 1984, after Tenzin had returned to Old Camp 1 in Bylakuppe. With three young children, two aging parents, and a husband away in the military, Tenzin was overwhelmed. She asked a settlement friend who worked in the governor's office to write a letter to the Indian army, pleading for the release of her husband.

The letter worked. In 1985, Migmar walked out of the army and headed to Bylakuppe. Tenzin was overjoyed. One year later, in the humid monsoon season of 1986, the couple celebrated the arrival of their youngest son, Tenzin Thardoe.

Three years passed. In 1989, Tenzin and Migmar began hearing rumors that a thousand Tibetan refugees from settlements in Nepal and India would be able to enter their names in a special US immigration lottery.

Tenzin, the young woman born and raised in the dusty, if successful, settlement, looked at her four small children and said to her husband, "Let's try."

By that time, more than one hundred and ten thousand refugees lived in forty-seven settlements sprawling across India and Nepal. One to two thousand more fled across China's borders each year, although the Indian government no longer made land allotments for these newcomers. Each Tibetan refugee family was allowed to submit only one name to the resettlement lottery. Families debated who could be spared and who had the best chance of being selected. From among fifteen thousand people who finally applied, the Central Tibetan Administration in Dharamsala carefully tried to choose a balance between new, often landless refugees who had come most recently from Tibet and those who had been in India and Nepal the longest; between people largely illiterate and those with education and special skills; between family heads and single persons. They looked for strong men and women, ages eighteen to forty-five.

Miraculously to Tenzin, her name was drawn.

"I was shocked. I was scared. At first I didn't want to go."

Neighbors crowded around the couple, urging them to accept, trying to explain the application process and the caveats.

In the United States, drafts of federal legislation to offer aid to the Tibetan cause had failed for years. But the 1990 Immigration Act, introduced by US Representative Barney Frank of Massachusetts, succeeded. The Central Tibetan Administration first identified six, then sixteen, then twenty-two US "cluster communities," coast to coast from Vermont to California and border to border from Minnesota to New Mexico, as well as Tibetan American or Tibet-knowledgeable leaders in each city. Many were university communities, some with already-established Tibetan Buddhist temples or cultural centers. The resettlement program was visionary, and small groups of Americans willing to help with initial housing, job contacts, and fund-raising stepped forward to welcome the arriving flights. Through my brief association with the Tibetan Resettlement Project in Madison, I was almost, but not quite, one of them.

In the United States, the question of what to call the newly arriving Tibetans had caused problems in the drafting of the legislation. They were not "asylum seekers" because that term would offend China, where Tibetans in the Tibet Autonomous Region (TAR) were regarded as ordinary Chinese citizens. But legislators balked at calling them "refugees" because that term in US bureaucratic language entitled individuals to federal assistance, however modest and brief. Nor could they be called normal "immigrants," because China, India, and Nepal were all oversubscribed for US immigration visas. So, in Section 123 of the 1990 Immigration Act, they became "qualified, displaced Tibetans." "Qualified" meant they were eligible for permanent residency in the United States and entitled to apply for American citizenship after five years. They were immediately eligible for a green card, the much sought-after permission to legally apply for and hold jobs. Unlike other refugees to the United States, however, the act stipulated they were entitled to no welfare assistance for three years and that the Tibetan United States Resettlement Project, however overdue, compassionate, and well intentioned, would receive no federal funds.

Tenzin didn't care what the legislation called her. Likewise, she had little awareness of the joy and relief felt by scores of people who had long lobbied for US involvement in the Tibetan cause. Still in India, Tenzin wrestled with her choice, to go or to stay. She looked to Migmar, who said calmly but firmly, "Let's stay. We have enough of everything here. We don't have much money, but we have enough food." Her parents and older sisters, concerned she would be leaving not only them but also four young children, agreed with Migmar. How could they manage without her? Yet other friends and neighbors envied her chance to be one of the "lucky one thousand."

Tenzin was bewildered by the urgency and enormity of the decision before her. As she delayed, the first groups began departing Bylakuppe, America-bound—batch one, batch two. It was time to make a choice.

CHAPTER 3

Migmar's Story

Be content with what you have, in the way things are. When you realize there is nothing lacking, the whole world belongs to you.

—Lao Tzu, ancient Chinese philosopher

Stories of community elders like Migmar are being collected by California's esteemed Tibet Oral History Project and translated and collected in places such as Case Western Reserve University's prestigious Tibetan Oral History Archives. The traditional way of life in tiny villages on the Tibetan plateaus has almost disappeared, as these eyewitnesses to turbulent history have grown older. To record his story, I asked Migmar questions, with the help of his more English-fluent children. His kids loved his story, parts of which they had heard many times. They would gather around us and shout translations and answers. "Let Migmar answer!" I insisted. Sometimes I would ask a question whose answer his children didn't know, and they would turn to him to listen.

❧

Migmar Dorjee was born at home in Lhading village, near the town of Samadha in the Ü-Tsang region of southern Tibet. He was the youngest of five children. Although Migmar's mother didn't record the date of his birth, he believes he was probably born in 1946. *Migmar* means "Tuesday" in Tibetan. His second name, Dorjee, comes from a Sanskrit word for an ancient Buddhist scepter that is still used in ceremonies today, its indestructibility symbolized by a diamond and thunderbolt. Like most Tibetans, Migmar does not use a surname, although he could have claimed Shiga, as his ancestors descended from the Shiga manorial estates.

Migmar recalls a carefree and easygoing childhood beneath a magnificent blue sky, with raptors floating overhead on thermal updrafts. A hundred houses made up the village. Migmar's family home was like the others, built of mud, two stories tall, with cows, yaks, a horse, and a donkey milling near the first-floor shelter, and the family's living quarters on the floor above. A skylight let the smoke escape and the sun shine in on the two sparsely furnished bedrooms and the two grain-filled storerooms. The family's hundred sheep roamed somewhere in the mountains, cared for by relatives who still lived in the centuries-old, nomadic way.

Early each morning, Migmar woke to the sound of his mother lighting a small branch of dry cedar as incense. While she performed prayers outside at the eight-foot-tall village altar, called a *nedhang*, he went about the house, waving incense in each room. For breakfast, the family ate *jamdhur*, which was barley flour mixed with hot water, and the ever-present hot butter tea, called *bjoeja*, which was a staple of the harsh, windy climate.

"Follow the yak, Migmar-lak," encouraged his oldest brother, Tenpa, as Migmar trotted alongside him during the spring plowing. "That's my first memory," Migmar told me, guessing he was then about four years old.

Until he was seven years old, Migmar ran and shrieked

through the village with the other children. With the neighbor kids, he played a Tibetan version of hide-and-seek, called dog and ram, or *khi dang thong*, in which the "rams" hid inside village houses, then scampered to the next house, with the "dog" in pursuit. Similar to marbles, in *dekhong*, children tossed one stone and tried to hit three other stones set in a line. While boys played *dekhong*, girls played jacks, or *apdho*, with five small rocks. One day Migmar's brother delighted him with a little bamboo flute, called *lingphu*, from a market in Gyantse, the next town over. For the rest of his life, Migmar found flutes to play, as his journeys took him farther and farther from Tibet.

These memories are in striking contrast to the cruelty happening in neighboring regions of Tibet. China's People's Liberation Army, or PLA, had invaded Tibet as early as 1949. In the years since then, the PLA had enforced widespread redistribution of the lands of noblemen and monasteries. The young Dalai Lama protested China's invasion; in 1951, he contested a Seventeen Point Agreement that established China's sovereignty over Tibet, signed under duress by a representative delegation that had journeyed to Beijing.

The agreement promised autonomy for Tibet and for Lhasa, Tibet's beautiful holy city and the seat of the young Dalai Lama's government. At first the Chinese army left the lands surrounding Lhasa largely in peace, including the area that encompassed Migmar's village, but claimed the neighboring eastern regions of Kham and Ando, renaming them Tsinghai, Szechwan, and Yunnan provinces. Stringent land reforms spread across the region, and as the PLA seized the fields of Tibetan monasteries and nobility, Chinese officials divided people into five strata. The top three strata suffered public humiliation or were turned over to firing squads. Chinese authorities imprisoned lamas and monks or condemned them to death after cursory or farcical trials.

From village to village, news spread of monks being murdered and monasteries destroyed, along with ancient libraries and revered icons of Buddhism. These reports bred mistrust and resentment toward Chinese soldiers that eventually turned into open resentment and hostility toward the Chinese people. From 1950 to 1959, historians document periodic but uncoordinated attacks, uprisings, rebellions, and guerrilla warfare by Tibetan peasants against the PLA.

As a young boy, Migmar had little awareness of the struggles happening on the other side of the mountains and rivers. When he was about seven, he and a neighbor boy named Tsering were given responsibility for the neighborhood's twenty cows. They went from house to house in the early mornings, coaxing the cows up the paths into the foothills, as far as the Drumpa Raptchu River, a village boundary. There the cows would find grass amongst the stones. The boys wove windmills from grass and built water wheels in the river.

Migmar and Tsering carried their lunches in small leather bags that closed with a double drawstring. Their lunch was often a doughy mixture of grain and butter, called *pak*, or a mash of roasted barley and water, which they ate with their fingers. Migmar's family raised all their food, including meat. When food at home was scarce, Migmar's bag contained only dry cheese (*churra*) and butter (*mar*) to keep hunger at bay, but on better days he might find in it a little lamb or yak meat.

The cows knew it was time to head home when the sun started to set. Migmar and Tsering returned the animals to their respective corrals before dashing off to play with younger village kids until it was time for supper, which looked much the same as breakfast.

Daily routines were punctuated only by an occasional remarkable storm, or by a birth, wedding, or death among the neighbors. Marriages were modest home affairs, not officiated by a monk, though a monk or lama would come to say prayers if someone in the family was sick. Each family sent one son, usually a middle child, to become a monk at Dayku Gonpa Monastery, five miles away. For Migmar's family, that was Namdol, the fourth-born, who set off for his life as a monk when he was ten years old.

For the first several years, Migmar told me, Namdol studied with boys his age, crowded together in a common room for sleeping, and sitting cross-legged on thin cushions in small groups for long hours of memorization and recitation. Several years later, Migmar's family was pleased to hear Namdol was scheduled to pass his examination of "collected topics" and be assigned his own room in the monastery. The family loaded their donkey with a table and chair, mattress, pillow, and clothing for Namdol, and tucked in a little money so he could afford a monk's maroon robe, shawl, and vest.

Village children who didn't go to the monastery were home-schooled, if they were schooled at all. From his older brother Tenpa, Migmar learned the flowing Tibetan script, something he still can write confidently. Once a week, a nomad woman who stayed in their village during the winters told stories to Migmar and his peers, as the children gathered around the woman's warm stove. Outside, the cold sun dried the piles of sheep manure the children had gathered for fuel for their own families' stoves. Today, Migmar struggles to remember these stories for his own children and grandchildren, stories such as "Tail Boy," "The Cow King," "The Two Step Brothers," and "Three Brothers and a King."

I could picture young Migmar, sitting, wide-eyed and giggling, as the old woman captivated the children with the rich, rambling, ribald stories that had been passed down. One story the family shared with me, "Tail Boy," follows the mischievous escapades of the living, talking tail of a sheep that an old man and an old woman had fought over and pulled apart. Over the course of the story, Tail Boy uses various ruses—involving a manure pile, the ear of a gray yak, a yak bladder, sheep stomach, and sleepy donkey—to fool the elderly man and woman, wealthy property owners, robbers, and even a wizard. Tibetan stories begin with the phrase "*Ngonma, ngonma*" (A long time ago) and end with a difficult-to-translate phrase that approximately means, "Old man Melted Butter Drop lived fat and happy." I looked in many indices of Tibetan folk tales but could not find Tail Boy. In Migmar's memory, Tail Boy rested contentedly in the lands he had cleverly tricked away from the rich merchant.

⁓

"Look! Look!" the children yelled.

Vehicles in Migmar's village were rare. In the distance a dust-covered PLA jeep spun red dirt into a dramatic storm cloud. By the time it reached Lhading and chugged to a halt, overheated and in need of water, even the adults had gathered to watch by the roadside. No one spoke, as the villagers and the Chinese soldiers had no common language. It was 1957; Migmar was about eleven years old.

In the months to come, more jeeps, then trucks, teeming with soldiers and supplies, would roar past his village into the neighboring town. One day the soldiers didn't continue onward; they stayed. In a big, open ground, they began holding daily education and disciplinary meetings. The uniformed Chinese officials identified and tied up wealthy individuals and town leaders and listed their faults. With translations spoken by a Tibetan who lived in a border town near China, the Chinese soldiers explained that rich people had been oppressing poor people for too many years; now it was their turn to be oppressed. They made the captured individuals bend over, yelled at them, and struck them with sticks, fists, or rifle butts.

"At first, the Tibetans liked the Chinese," Migmar told me through his children's translations. "They provided the adults jobs with salaries and a chance, for the first time, to be a supervisor. And we knew it was true, many of these rich people had been mean to us."

That first year, the soldiers kept coming, and they marched up and down through the streets and gathered in small groups. Gradually, however, not only town leaders but also ordinary people living in the village were targeted for discipline. By then, no fewer than twenty thousand PLA troops had moved into central Tibet. The violence continued to spread, and in March 1959, ten thousand to fifteen thousand Tibetans were killed within three days in Lhasa. Resistance grew throughout Tibet. Adding to the duress of the year, Migmar's father died of old age.

When they heard stories of their beloved monks being tortured in the neighboring monastery, the people of Migmar's village could no longer wait. One by one, families escaped. They fled without telling their closest neighbors or saying good-bye to lifetime friends, since they did not know who had been recruited as paid informers. Sometimes, if someone became sick or word didn't reach a relative in time to join the departing family, planned dates were delayed.

Migmar's eldest brother Tenpa's position as town councilman of Lhading village and Tsamardok township marked him as a target of the PLA. When the family learned that Tenpa was scheduled for discipline, they began their preparations to leave in earnest, in a countdown against the date of Tenpa's public shaming. The family knew that two weeks were barely enough time to notify Namdol to come home from the monastery, prepare the grains needed for travel, and sew packs for twenty yaks and the eleven people in their traveling party: Migmar's family, his brother Tenpa's family, and his sister Migkyi's family. They divided the yaks into three groups. In the first-floor stables of their homes they readied loads of blankets, two tents, and a week's worth of roasted barley, constantly worried a neighbor would notice and report their extra activity.

At 2 a.m. on an overcast night in December 1959, the three families crept out their back doors as the village slept. They led their burdened yaks as quietly as they could through two feet of snow, heading toward the foothills, gorges, and ridges that rose quickly into the Himalayas beyond. The falling snow soon whipped into a fierce blizzard, blinding them so they could not look back on the village they would never see again, but obscuring their tracks from any Chinese soldiers who might discover their absence. They headed in the direction of Bhutan.

In the hour before their departure, Tenpa's wife gave Migmar a handful of moistened, roasted barley. "Put this in your coat pocket," she told him. Hours later, when Migmar complained he was hungry, she reminded him, "Eat your *tsampa*." He put his hand in his pocket, but it was empty. As he had stumbled and fallen in the snow in the early morning darkness, the small ball of grain must have dropped out.

Despite the blizzard, they kept looking backward. Migmar's sister Migkyi, her husband, and her husband's older parents should have caught up with them at the edge of the village. Migmar's family assumed the elders were slowing the group down.

As they reached the summit, the blizzard became life-threatening, with screaming winds that hurled blinding chunks of ice and snow. Landmarks disappeared. The group decided to turn back to Sammar, a village through which they had just passed, praying the storm might slow down any soldiers in pursuit. In the confusion of turning around, seven of their yaks not only turned but kept on descending back toward their home in the valley. The gray-and-black beasts disappeared into the whiteness, carrying not just food and blankets, but all of the family's wealth—silver and copper coins and heirloom jewelry of silver, amber, and turquoise.

In Sammar, the men yanked out and tied up the single tent that remained, its hand-sewn edges flapping furiously in the wind. Exhausted, Migmar fell asleep inside the tent, his head on his mother's lap, while the men slept outside sitting up, in relentless, blowing snow.

In the morning they still saw no sign of Migkyi and her group. Heartbroken, the family faced the probability that Migkyi had been captured by the PLA. It would be five decades before Migmar would learn what happened to her.

Migmar's legs were so frozen from the brutal night in the cramped position that he could not walk. Namdol lifted him atop a yak. High above the blowing snow, the thirteen-year-old rode over the crest of the Himalayas and into the Kingdom of Bhutan, toward an uncertain future.

∼

As they headed down the mountains in the following days, other fleeing families emerged out of the whiteness, and their numbers grew to ragged strings of travelers. With a dozen here and a hundred there, more than eighty thousand people fled from Tibet that first year. Their eventual destination was Dharamsala, India, as they followed the footsteps of their revered leader, His Holiness the Fourteenth Dalai Lama, who had escaped just a month earlier.

The climate on the backside of the Himalayas changed rapidly. They stumbled over the jagged pass and frozen tundra to flatter rocky expanses, then alpine meadows, and finally into subtropical forests of Bhutan, called the Land of Thunder and Dragons. They sweated, even shivered, in the extreme humidity, parched with thirst, swatting insects they had never seen before. The heat was not just oppressive but terrifying for people who had lived a lifetime in a cold climate. Among the tens of thousands of refugees, children and older people succumbed in large numbers.

As the monthlong trek dragged on, Migmar's older brothers sold one of the remaining yaks for food and bought a mule. They killed another yak for meat, yet still they were forced to beg food from the Bhutanese people whose small homes they passed. The Bhutanese peasants were sympathetic, sharing their religion and their prayers, and they helped the passersby when they could. Even the refugees could see these kind people were barely eking out a living. Though some Tibetans remained to settle among them, Migmar's family continued past the isolated yak herders' encampments, toward India.

For Migmar, the next years were filled with upheaval and uncertainty. Without a country, citizenship, an education, a job, or money, how was a young man to make a life? Thousands of his countrymen were asking the same question.

In Assam, India, Migmar's family joined a crowd of other refugees who had crammed into a big hall, where each family was assigned a few square meters in a long, quickly erected shelter. As 1959 crossed to 1960, Migmar's family reached Dharamsala in time to celebrate the New Year, or *Losar*. Their prayers were especially fervent.

~

Gravely concerned about the ill health and despair of the ever-increasing crowds, Tibetan and Indian government officials soon split the refugees into work teams of forty or fifty and packed them off on trains. Each group was assigned a different destination and task: to build roads and dams, to begin clearing land for transit camps, or to construct temporary buildings.

Migmar's family was first sent to Bobina, eight hundred miles south in the Indian state of Uttar Pradesh, and assigned to build roads. The adults toiled from morning to evening, seven days a week, while teens like Migmar were put to work as water boys. He and a new friend, Gyatso, balanced yokes on their shoulders, picking their way down steep mountain paths, twice in the morning and twice in the afternoon, to bring water from the river in the valley back up to the workers. Young and strong, the boys climbed trees between their shifts.

The Tibetan adults, men and women side by side, performed backbreaking labor, digging through stone without dynamite or machinery, pickaxes and wheelbarrows their only tools. Paltry nutrition and poor sanitation, together with the hard work, made them susceptible to tuberculosis and typhoid. In the evenings after a scant meal they cooked for themselves, one of the adults would gather the children together in a tent and, in the remaining single hour of light, conduct a Tibetan language class. Migmar was delighted; at age fourteen, this was his first schooling with other children. Then all settled to sleep in the dark tent city, as there were no candles or kerosene.

As the numbers of refugees mounted, the fledgling Tibetan government-in-exile struggled for solutions to many problems, among them how to educate so many children, and, now that they were far from Tibet, how to teach them their language, religion, and traditions.

After Migmar had spent a short time at the tent school, his mother and the other parents were told to send their children back to Dharamsala. For three months Migmar studied in a single classroom crowded with forty other students of all ages and grades. Eventually the Tibetan officials opened a proper school for refugee children in Mussoorie, an abandoned British colonial hill station in the cooler north Indian district of Dehradun, which was serving as the initial quarters for the Dalai Lama and the exiled government.

Despite his age, Migmar was formally placed in first grade.

Tutored by strict male and female Tibetan teachers, he studied Tibetan language, the Tibetan Buddhist religion, English, math, science, and social studies. Highly motivated to learn, Migmar completed five years of schooling in four years. He was intensely homesick the whole time, allowed to travel by train to see his family only once in the four years.

His family's progress was as remarkable as his own. They were no longer in Bobina. They had been among the initial group of refugees who had responded to the state of Karnataka's invitation for three thousand settlers, and they had headed south by rail to Bylakuppe, near the city of Mysore. While Migmar studied in Mussoorie, his older brothers cleared the dense forest to create farmland, encountered elephants and tigers still at large, and struggled through several years of crop failures. In those early days, the brothers would have paid little notice to married women gathering water or struggling to plant their own fields. They wouldn't have noticed that one of them, Pema Choedon, was carrying a baby named Tenzin Kelsang strapped to her back as she worked, destined one day to become their youngest brother's wife.

Too soon for Migmar, his days of schooling ended. The Indian Ministry of Education took the Mussoorie school under its purview and dismissed the older students.

Migmar was deeply disappointed. He and nine other students were sent to a poorly run, minimally funded Boyston Technical High School near Hyderabad, in south India. It was the first time Migmar had encountered the mixed-race, multilingual, multireligious Catholic, Hindu, and Muslim youth in whose country he now lived. The Tibetan teens made friends with the other students, joining them to play soccer on the school's field and, on weekends, to swim in Hussain Sagar, Hyderabad's big, heart-shaped lake. They couldn't afford to rent boats on the lake, but for the equivalent of fifty cents, they could rent bikes for a full day. Boarding school food was bad, just two *chipati* (flat bread) for breakfast and a single scoop of oats and rice, mixed with watery yogurt, for lunch and supper. With so much dry food in stock, small bugs crawled onto the daily menu too, and students gingerly flicked bugs out of their bowls, wrinkling their faces in disgust.

Even worse was the curriculum. Instead of learning a trade, Migmar and the other carpentry students made wooden nails. "We were slaves," Migmar scoffed.

Knowing they were entitled to a better education, the refugee students complained to Tibetan officials in Bylakuppe, where their families lived, over their winter break. They begged, to no avail, to be allowed to go back to school in Mussoorie. Sent back once again to Hyderabad, they began complaining regularly to the local Indian welfare officer, and finally, with indignation, left the school to register a formal complaint at the regional Tibetan education offices in Delhi. Without money for train fare, just five rupees among the ten of them, they went without food for two days on the train and deftly hid from the ticket takers. Upon arrival, they used a little money to implore two rickshaw drivers to take them to downtown Delhi. Walking into the education building with a demand for quality schooling, they definitely startled the regional bureaucrat. He told them they had no choice to attend elsewhere; the Central Tibetan Administration had already paid their tuition.

Even today, Migmar would love the chance for more schooling. He has an eager mind and a good memory, and he marvels at the education available to his children in the United States. A young man of different means in Migmar's day might have ended up in law or medical school, but for a Tibetan refugee student—not even a citizen of India—who lacked money or status, the Indian military was waiting and willing.

Young Tibetan men such as Migmar became part of the five-thousand-strong Indo-Tibetan Border Patrol that was eventually heralded for bravery in the Indo-Pakistani War. Tibetan soldiers, forced by China from the country of their birth, marched from border to border, defending India against those who might attack from Pakistan or Bangladesh.

"When are we going to fight our own war?" Tibetan refugee soldiers asked one another. And though high-ranking Tibetan and Indian officials sometimes discussed it, there would be no action against China for Migmar's unit.

In his twenty years as a soldier, from 1965 to 1985, Migmar advanced from telegraph set operator to sergeant, then weapon and drill inspector, and finally to quarter master, supervising rations for 120 Tibetan men. In his free time, he taught himself to play various flutes, to sew, to tailor, and to speak fluent Hindi. Years later, after a formal appeal from Tenzin to return to his responsibilities as father and husband, he left for Bylakuppe without lump-sum payment or pension.

One could see how a man might be happy to live out his remaining days in the settlement known as Old Camp 1, driving tractors in the farming cooperative, enjoying his children who were born in his absence, and sharing recollections with his brothers and other men who had marched over the Himalayas as boys. After years of turmoil, Migmar's family—and the religion, language, music, dance, foods, and traditions that thousands of Tibetans had fled to preserve—were all around him.

But Migmar's stamina would be called upon for yet another journey, to climb different kinds of mountains, and to dream of a better education, this time not for himself, but for his children.

CHAPTER 4

~

Becoming Friends

There are no strangers here, only friends you haven't yet met.
—WILLIAM BUTLER YEATS, IRISH POET

Tenzin's decision to join those leaving for the United States was incremental. Each time she expressed confusion and hesitation, settlement officials assured her they would walk her through the steps and help her document her family's vaccination records, birth dates, and employment history.

On a bright March day in 1993, she boarded a plane in Delhi, reassured by the excited, nervous chatter of her forty or so fellow travelers. From their stop and overnight in Aman, Jordan, many left for other countries. She remembers feeling exhausted and surprised that the journey went on and on, with another night spent in New York, another flight to Washington, DC, then a trip by car with host families to Virginia. By that point, the big group had been reduced to just four. She settled into a small bedroom in the house where she would be a live-in housekeeper for a Charleston couple and their children.

~

Until Tenzin's children and husband arrived in Madison, I wouldn't have called us best friends or even good friends. She was simply someone in my life. Yet our relationship wasn't limited to her pop-in appearances in my cubicle. Over time we began to socialize outside of work. Tenzin had a generous, engaging spirit, and I was fascinated by how easy it was to connect, as women, in a world that had dealt us such different hands.

During those years before Tenzin's family arrived, I had what I considered the best state job in Wisconsin. I felt lucky to be paid for duties I might willingly have done as a volunteer. I was the state's first international education consultant, a position created by State Superintendent of Public Instruction Herbert Grover and three visionary colleagues who saw the necessity of preparing Wisconsin's K-12 students and teachers to participate in globally connected communities. At the office, my workday might include a visiting delegation of teachers from Japan, Germany, Thailand, Mexico, or the Republic of Georgia. During my time working at the Department of Public Instruction, three separate governors welcomed international delegations with receptions in the governor's mansion. We created an International Education Council of globally minded academics and community leaders. We wrote one of the nation's first state-published curriculum guides linking K–12 subjects to global issues. Waves of young teachers from Japan, more than two hundred of them over the sixteen years I worked there, arrived for placement in elementary, middle, and high schools around the state. We took our Japanese teachers to visit American Indian communities in Lac du Flambeau and Menominee, where Native elders sang and youth showed powwow steps, and in exchange, the Japanese teachers taught students Tanko Bushi, the coal miners' dance, and how to fold origami peace cranes.

Work with constantly changing groups from abroad involved striking a balance between respect for the visitors' customs and the creation of a shared bilateral protocol. For example, I remember one meeting in Madison with a delegation of education ministry officials from Japan. I arranged for four translators, English to Japanese and Japanese to English, two for the visiting delegation and two for our state education team. I had briefed the Wisconsin meeting participants on Japanese protocols of greeting. Yet many of us smiled when the Americans bowed while simultaneously the Japanese extended their hands for a handshake. The appreciation I developed for flexibility in bicultural spaces would serve me well.

I embraced the challenges of my work and the fascinating cultural study I saw as necessary, not just for me, but for all of Wisconsin's teachers and students, to undertake. Operating where the rules were unformed or fluid taught me the courage to push past the initial awkwardness when people from different backgrounds gathered. That's not to say I didn't make errors, but I found most educators in such situations to be understanding, their criticism gentle and suggestions tentative.

Tenzin's workdays during those years were less glamorous. When the first eighty-eight Tibetan newcomers arrived in Madison from India and Nepal in 1993, family sponsors and organizers of the Tibetan Resettlement Project helped them find jobs. A prominent hotel in the center of Madison's downtown was among the first to step forward to offer work, willing to overlook some newcomers' lack of high school education or rudimentary English. At the same time, it also overlooked other newcomers' advanced educational and professional backgrounds. Everyone accepted this, if reluctantly, as their immediate necessity was to earn money to support their families.

Tenzin promptly landed a job cleaning rooms at the hotel, taken under the wing of previously arrived Tibetans who had already established a reputation as hardworking, punctual, and respectful employees. Tenzin was evaluated on how quickly she cleaned, checking off a list of twenty-five tasks per room, from dusting bulbs, baseboards, and vent slats to sorting and washing the color-coded cleaning rags, each designated for a different task. She usually cleaned fifteen hotel rooms in her seven-hour day, attending to the 375 checklist details, and earned $4.75 an hour.

"How many guests leave a tip for maid service?" I asked her once, about her work at the hotel.

"Tip?" she repeated. "What's a tip?"

A manager's assistant opened up the rooms that needed cleaning, she explained, and none of the maids ever saw a tip. Hearing that, I started hiding my own tips under a bed pillow or under a coffeepot when staying at hotels for my job. Tenzin and the other housekeepers talked among themselves, and after a few inquiries to their supervisor, they started finding tips—"one in twenty rooms," she answered my question some months later.

Tenzin's take-home pay of $166 per week wasn't enough to cover her bills. So she joined a crew contracted to clean state office buildings, including the one where I worked, beginning at 5 p.m. and ending at 9 p.m. It paid five dollars an hour and was a ten-minute walk from her day job at the hotel. All the workers on the crew had other jobs, either day jobs or third shift. Crew members often didn't share the same language, so they merely nodded as they passed in the halls, each assigned an entire floor to herself. Invisible to the day employees, they moved cubicle to cubicle in the silent buildings. The work was difficult by any standard, and the multiple shifts made their days exhausting. The low status of the work cast an additional shadow, especially over those who had worked in India and Nepal as venerated monks, high-ranking administrators, or respected school principals, university professors, or artists.

Between the hotel and the office building, Tenzin cleaned as many as 25 toilets a day, perhaps 120 in a week, all with cleansers containing sodium hypochlorite—bleach—that left welts extending from her wrists to her shoulders. I was shocked to see the red abrasions. I had never thought of a cleaning job as dangerous.

A fellow Tibetan American on the cleaning crew informed Tenzin that a local hospital needed cleaners, so she signed on for a Saturday afternoon shift from 3:30 to 9 p.m. On Sundays she cleaned a church in her neighborhood after services let out at noon. Her weekends had much the same rhythm as weekdays; only the locations changed. At least her weekend pay was better, eight dollars an hour.

Tenzin's working hours now totaled sixty-two per week, and her monthly take-home pay had risen to sixteen hundred dollars per month. In 1995, with a tip from another Tibetan American acquaintance, she traded her hotel job for an eight-dollar-an-hour daytime cleaning job at Kennedy Manor, an older, redbrick apartment building near the state capitol. Kennedy Manor's charm, lake views, and dining room attracted graduate students and politicians who needed an apartment when the legislature was in session. Tenzin's "office" was in the basement laundry next to the boiler room, cozy in winter but stifling in summer.

While Tenzin worked days, nights, and weekends, my days, in contrast, brimmed with opportunity and stimulation. I folk danced on weekends, biked on rural roads, swam in forest lakes, and had potluck dinners with friends I had known for decades. I delighted in movies by independent filmmakers, attended folk music concerts, and met acquaintances for ice cream on the University of Wisconsin's legendary Memorial Union Terrace. In those years I was renting a charming lakeside cottage across from the university, its original logs from Wisconsin's pre-statehood governor James Doty, who had used it as a fishing cabin. The cottage stuck out on a tiny promontory, so I reveled in both sunrises and sunsets. My friends adored it, and I hosted parties, picnics, and potlucks almost weekly.

In those early years, when I introduced Tenzin to my friends at one of these gatherings, she would physically turn away, ducking her head and smiling in shyness. One on one, however, she was an attentive listener and a charming conversationalist with an engaging sense of humor.

An acquaintance named Terry was known among my friends as a self-made millionaire before he had turned thirty. He and Tenzin sat together in lawn chairs at an afternoon picnic at my cottage, and I overheard Terry explaining to Tenzin that the wages he paid the cleaning staff in his corporate motel chain were adequate, if perhaps low, since in addition, the house-keepers received tips. After all, Terry said, most of his employees had other jobs, and these cleaning jobs provided additional wages. Tenzin threw back her head and laughed. She described how much she earned at her multiple cleaning jobs, how much she paid in rent and for food. Terry countered her, but Tenzin held her ground: a person could not live in Madison on a motel maid's monthly wages.

Carrying out dessert and wine, I passed by them again. This time Tenzin was conversationally asking Terry if he knew how many representatives and senators we had. She was studying for her citizenship test and had been surprised that many Americans didn't know the answers. Tenzin and Terry sat for a good hour together, two of Madison's richest and poorest citizenry, looking out over the waves and sailboats, discussing the structure of the US economy and government.

～

Tenzin's childhood hadn't offered opportunities to learn to swim or to ride a bike, much less to cross-country ski or to canoe winding rivers. In those days I was unaware it might cost her two days of wages just to come along on one of my carefree weekend adventures. She gingerly climbed into a canoe for a Memorial Day outing on the Wisconsin River with me and others who came every year to my friend Jack's country place near Woodman, Wisconsin. Kestrels and red-tailed hawks flew overhead. The current and winds were mellow, and Tenzin, bundled in her head scarf and life jacket, finally relaxed as the currents flowed lazily. She marveled over cirrus clouds that patterned the turquoise sky, great blue herons and snowy egrets poised in the shallows, and fat turtles that splashed off glistening logs.

I asked her recently if she remembered that weekend. "I was scared lotta things," she told me. "I didn't know how to paddle. Paddle, paddle! I worried the canoe might tip over. Your friends told me, 'Stay away from the poison ivy,' but I didn't know what is poison ivy. I tried to stay away from everything."

~

"Invite your friend," my friends began to add, as they extended to me various invitations to dinners, movies, and outings. By then I knew lots of Tenzins, but it did not seem to be an easy-to-remember name for others.

Colleagues often said things like, "You are so kind to her," or "It's so nice of you to include her." I winced at suggestions that Tenzin was my charity case or that she was not one of "us." I truly enjoyed her company and valued her refreshing perspectives, and I hoped my friends might include her in other social events, even without me, but somehow my presence always seemed necessary.

Nevertheless, I knew little about Tenzin's life those first five years. I had no way of knowing that her family would come to play a bigger part in my life. In truth, they would not be my first "adopted family." I had a dear host family or two in Sweden from my fellowship year in 1977–1978, and three families, all with kids, whom I had visited often during my three years in Japan, 1985–1988. In 1994, I had found a warm, incredible family with five kids in Senegal, West Africa. Within the generous embrace of hospitality of these families, I began unraveling mysteries of the culture and learning the language. I felt accepted, centered, and expansive in their midst.

Tenzin introduced me to her Tibetan acquaintances in Madison as her sponsor. In immigration terminology, a sponsor is a person who commits substantive support for an individual and is liable for expenses, including possible health care and medical emergencies. In actuality, I was not her sponsor, merely a curious, interested, occasional companion, fascinated with cultural differences and regretful on the topic of children.

One day she appeared at my desk, flustered, her eyes red and swollen.

"Can you help me get a visa? I need to go home right now. My mother is very sick."

Terribly busy, I procrastinated briefly, then made some phone calls and tried to fill out documents for a non-citizen to travel. Weeks passed. Her mother died. Tenzin was disconsolate, unable to help arrange memorial services or join her family to grieve. I felt helpless, unqualified, bewildered.

Still, month by month, the arrival of Tenzin's husband and children crept nearer: formal applications, tearful phone calls across the Atlantic Ocean, then a series of near misses as departure dates were scheduled then inexplicably delayed. Tenzin's anticipation was contagious. I was sure I could help out in the beginning days and especially help the kids get started in school. After all, education was my profession. Maybe after a year or so they would be well adjusted, and I would go on about my life. Again, I had it wrong.

CHAPTER 5

Four Children

Your children are not your children. They are the sons and daughters of Life's longing for itself. They came through you but not from you and though they are with you yet they belong not to you.

—KHALIL GIBRAN, LEBANESE AMERICAN
POET AND WRITER

On the night of March 8, 1998, Tenzin's family was scheduled to arrive in Madison—after flights from Delhi to Paris and Paris to Chicago, then a bus from Chicago to Madison. So much work and emotion had led to this moment. I had helped Tenzin fill out myriad forms and open bank accounts; sympathized with her tearful laments when she was overcome with loneliness; and chuckled at her glee as she described Goodwill purchases stacking up in a corner of her shared apartment. Now that the day had arrived, I was focused entirely on Tenzin's anticipation and the tremendous difference her family's arrival would make in her life, little aware that change was hurtling my way as well.

I had called two taxis to meet us at the bus stop in Madison to ferry them and their luggage to their new apartment. As I knocked on the window of one of the cabs, I could see my breath in the dark, cold air of a lingering Wisconsin winter.

"So you'll wait, right?" I confirmed with the driver.

Tenzin and her niece Karma had left early that morning by bus to meet the family at Chicago's O'Hare International Airport, then ride back with them to Madison. Karma was undoubtedly remembering the trepidation of her own arrival in Madison, just two years earlier, carrying her three-year-old son, ready to reunite with her husband, who had been one of the earlier arrivals. For Tenzin's family, a stack of firsts would be piled atop these two jet-lagged travel days: the family's departure from India, their first time in an airplane, their first transatlantic flight, their reunion with mother and wife after six years spent largely apart, and my first chance to meet Tenzin's family.

About 9:30 p.m. the bus pulled in and seven silhouettes carefully disembarked. I recognized Tenzin and Karma, who greeted me eagerly. Then all three of us turned to watch as Migmar Dorjee stepped off the bus. Next came four slender children, ages eleven to sixteen, almost all the same height—first Namgyal Tsedup, the oldest son, then Nawang Lhadon, the family's only girl. Tenzin Tamdin, the second son, looked around curiously, and finally, Tenzin Thardoe, the youngest, tall and slender. Even in the dimness, I could see his eager grin.

They all helped to shove ten enormous cargo bags and five backpacks into Karma's husband's SUV. I hadn't known her husband was coming. At the last minute, Tenzin had also requested the bus driver to call ahead to order two taxis. Had she worried I would forget to meet her? While I ran around, dismissing and tipping four annoyed, no-longer-needed cab drivers, the four kids, Migmar, and Karma happily crammed into the SUV, sitting atop luggage piles, no matter about seat belts. Flustered and already trying to micromanage the way I thought things were supposed to happen in my country, I tapped Tenzin on the shoulder as she, too, was climbing into the crowded van and coaxed her to ride with me. She kindly, if reluctantly, stepped into my front seat to follow the van to the family's new apartment.

That year, 1998, Madison's small Tibetan refugee population more than quadrupled, from its eighty-eight original arrivals assigned in the first lottery batches, plus add-ons like Tenzin, to about four hundred. True sponsors, the Tibetan Americans themselves rather than Madison volunteers, had helped one another with the confusing, detailed family reunification applications, often while living crowded together, four adults in one- and two-bedroom apartments. As they waited for their families to join them, they worked multiple jobs, lived frugally to save money, improved their English skills, and gathered furnishings, preparing for momentous days just like this one.

~

I watched as Tenzin unlocked the door to their new apartment in a less-affluent neighborhood on Madison's East Side. The kids stepped in and were completely quiet. They peered intently at the living room furnishings and marched in single file down a carpeted hallway to their shared bedroom, with its double sets of Goodwill-purchased bunk beds. Then all four ran back into the living room and dove onto the plush sofa with squeals of delight, jumped on and off a couple of times, then snuggled into its velvety throw pillows.

Later Tenzin showed me an old snapshot of the family's three-room house in Bylakuppe, with its tiny kitchen and woodstove and a room in which parents slept in one bed and the four kids all slept together on two single beds, pushed together to make one. Comparatively, I thought the new apartment would seem luxurious.

After they left Bylakuppe, however, the children and their father had waited for months in Delhi for their US immigration papers to clear. While there, they saw the American film *Home Alone*. All four children imagined that in the United States, they, too, would have a three-story mansion like the one in the movie, complete with a swimming pool, billiard table, and treehouse.

Namgyal, the oldest, told me this a half year later.

"How soon did you figure out that wasn't going to happen?" I asked.

"As soon as we arrived in our apartment," he replied. I recalled that brief moment of silence when they had entered their new home and their quiet walk down the hall to the bedroom. They had successfully hidden their disappointment.

~

Because Tibetan naming conventions mean that common first names such as Tenzin are often repeated within a family, many Tibetans informally call each other by either their first or their second name. Though I didn't yet know about Tibetan names, I simply began calling the children by the names their parents used for them: Namgyal, Lhadon, Tamdin, and Thardoe. The four of them were shy with me for five minutes before erupting into gales of self-conscious giggles as they answered my questions about their flight and their first impressions of the world outside Bylakuppe. They spoke limited English with a British accent, as learned in their schoolrooms in India. Tenzin translated between us.

Poised and thoughtful Tamdin, the second son, told me that he and his best friend, Pema, had anticipated the family's departure for months. When their plane flew over Bylakuppe, Tamdin planned to roll down the window and throw out all of his Indian rupees, which he would no longer need in America.

Pema would be waiting down below to catch the money. Tamdin had peered closely as the plane took off and headed north toward Europe, coins and wrinkled bills in his fist, but he never saw his small southern Indian village. There was another problem, he told me, laughing at his naivety. "The windows wouldn't open."

The children had never eaten a Western-style salad, and they felt insulted when the flight attendant brought dinner trays containing bowls of lettuce and fresh vegetables.

"This is cow food!" Lhadon whispered to her father, and the children glared at the flight attendant.

In the confusing hustle and bustle of Charles de Gaulle International Airport, where they had to transfer to a Paris-to-Chicago flight, the family had been terrified of missing their plane. They were traveling with a group of twenty other displaced Tibetans in the process of US resettlement. Even though the wait at Charles de Gaulle was a full twelve hours, the adults in the group sat patiently at the assigned gate. Small children, who had never before seen an escalator, rode up and down, up and down, for hours.

Many ups and downs were still to come, not just for them but for me too.

I had gone to Goodwill and purchased four red sweatshirts with "University of Wisconsin" emblazoned across them, together with the university mascot, a feisty Bucky Badger. I put one on each of the four bunk beds before their arrival. I never saw the kids wear the sweatshirts, and Tenzin never thanked me for them. They were not new, and no one in the family at that point knew or cared who "Bucky Badger" was. As a relatively affluent middle-class white woman, I loved secondhand stores and imagined I was saving Tenzin's family money and giving her perfectly good items, culturally appropriate to Madison. I, of course, had the option of buying brand-new items—for myself and also as gifts for my friends. In retrospect, I wondered if Tenzin had been curious, or even insulted, that her "sponsor" hadn't honored her family with items newly purchased.

~

Over the first few months, I was startled by the many cultural differences both parents and children experienced on a daily basis. Something as simple as filling out new address forms or city health records with "Last Name, First Name" was a conundrum. The ancient and complex Tibetan naming traditions, in which each name held an auspicious meaning and was given to a child by a religious leader, was trumped by the American necessity for a surname. The four teens, and most other Tibetan Americans, simply used their "second name" when they filled in the "last name" box on ubiquitous forms. It would be as if I suddenly began using my middle name, Anne, as my last name.

When I tried to relay this interesting cultural mismatch to the public health nurses, school secretaries, or bank tellers, I was greeted with frowns of impatience. Nonetheless, for the benefit of the mail carrier, I pinned a list of names above the family's mailbox: Migmar Dorjee, Tenzin Kalsang, Namgyal Tsedup, Lhadon Nawang, Tenzin Tamdin, Tenzin Thardoe. They were six related people in one family. There was no last name.

Madison schools were deep in the academic year when the kids arrived, headed for summer vacation in just a few months. Tenzin requested time off from her job a couple of days later, and we loaded the children into my car to drive them to the nearest school for registration.

As I walked through the doors of Georgia O'Keefe Middle School with our entourage, a big worry troubled me: how would they catch up with their English-speaking peers? A second worry followed: would they lose their ties to Tibet?

In addition to the differences in schools between two continents and cultures, the children had the disadvantage of having missed a full year of schooling in India. As they had waited for visa clearances in Delhi while living with relatives, the date of their departure got postponed time and again. Lhadon dismissed my concern with a child's innocence, cheerfully explaining, "It didn't matter. We knew we would go to school in America."

Directed to sit in desks in an empty classroom, Tenzin, the children, and I waited to speak to the middle school principal. When he entered the room, he asked the kids' ages and began assigning them to area schools. Namgyal, he said, would start ninth grade at East High School. I panicked, imagining easygoing Namgyal, who barely spoke English, navigating his way among peers preparing for college entrance exams, taking Advanced Placement classes, or delving into sophisticated electives that Madison's public schools offered, such as anthropology, statistics, even aeronautics. I pleaded with the principal: couldn't Namgyal spend at least a year in middle school?

I was thinking in terms of academics; the principal was thinking along the lines of adolescent development. "There is absolutely no way a young man sixteen years old is going to be in this school with younger girls and boys," he said firmly.

Despite their missing year, the principal placed Tamdin and Lhadon in eighth grade, since they were the age of eighth graders. He directed Thardoe, age eleven, to register in the fifth grade at nearby Lowell Elementary School. Thardoe knew less English than his siblings, but he somehow managed to make it through the rest of the school year.

That summer, Thardoe attended the elementary school's remedial reading class. One day I stopped by to visit his classroom. Tall even for his age, Thardoe sat at a tiny table on a tiny chair, his knees practically up to his chin. Around him, small second graders laboriously read aloud from the children's book *Make Way for Ducklings*. Most teachers in the English as a Second Language program had in their classrooms whole bookshelves of easy, age-appropriate, action-and-adventure stories for teens learning English. That particular summer, however, since no ESL classes were available for students his age, Thardoe read about ducklings. "Before you could wink an eyelash," he slowly read aloud, "Jack, Kack, Lack, Mack, Nack, Ouack, Pack, and Quack fell into line, just as they had been taught." Since his school in India had taught English by repetition, not phonetically, sounding out each word was a struggle. He didn't seem to mind spending the morning among the smaller children, however, and he willingly went to school each day.

I kept expecting Thardoe and his siblings to be more rebellious or surly. I marveled over their smiles, their respect for their elders, and their cheerful demeanors. Inside, however, each was struggling with the new school experiences in different ways. For example, Tamdin, the second son, quickly grew frustrated in his middle school classes. The idea that a classroom could be noisy, with students on task, engaged in hands-on learning, working in small groups, upset him. He expected the teachers to beat misbehaving students as they had in India. This was not "school" as he knew it, and his brothers and sister agreed. Their classrooms in India had been quiet ones, with only the teacher talking. They had recited in unison, shared the few textbooks, and kept their desks in neat rows. They had all received handsome certificates for perfect attendance.

Tamdin's ESL teacher remembers many times observing him struggling with assignments, no longer the top student as he had been in India in schools run by the Tibetan Administration. One day she watched him use a pair of scissors to systematically and belligerently pound holes into a piece of Styrofoam. On another day he jumped up, hurled his desk onto its side, and stormed out of the room. Through the classroom window, the teacher kept an eye on him as he sat alone on a swing, pushing off with his feet.

For all four kids, ESL classes became a temporary cocoon, set apart from the school's regular—much less "talented and gifted" or advanced—college prep classes. Madison's ESL program served students who spoke ninety-eight languages, from elementary to high school. The parents of these students had many different reasons that brought them to Madison, from political asylum to prestigious university fellowships.

ESL classes provided a road map for Namgyal, Lhadon, Tamdin, and Thardoe to catch up with their peers. ESL students were called ELLs, or English-language learners. The classes focused on helping students acquire particular academic vocabulary and tools for succeeding in school, such as English for mathematics, English for science, and even English for learning English in the regular classes. After a year or two of ESL instruction, the siblings would be ready to move into regular classes, at first with the support of bilingual resource specialists, who would help them with vocabulary, concepts, and assignments. Namgyal's bilingual resource specialist at the high school spoke Spanish and English; the school did not the luxury of having a specialist for all of the languages spoken by students.

Tamdin's middle school ESL class that first year included two other Tibetan boys who had also recently arrived in Madison. Together, they were Tenzin Tamdin, Tenzin Wangmo, and Tenzin Wangyal. A Spanish-speaking boy in their class joked, "I'm Tenzin Pedro." Because of the mix of students in his ESL class, Tamdin's Spanish vocabulary expanded right along with his English.

～

Like the children, the parents straddled bilingual encounters too. When Migmar arrived, Tenzin, who had been working at Kennedy Manor for four years, convinced the manager to hire her husband as well. Tenzin dusted and vacuumed the apartments. Migmar emptied trash cans and barrels. They both polished brass on the antique Otis elevators, their brilliance, caught in sunlight, out of place in the dark halls.

Tenzin and Migmar became staples of good cheer and reliable punctuality. Every day from 8 a.m. to 1 p.m., they greeted residents as they passed in the halls. They knew everyone's names, and the residents knew theirs. A few residents were curious about their background. Others mistakenly greeted them in Spanish.

"*Buenos días*, Tenzin," an elderly gentleman always said.

"*Buenos días*," answered Tenzin. "*¿Cómo estás?*"

To their mornings at Kennedy Manor, Migmar and Tenzin added better-paid, union-supported cleaning jobs at the University of Wisconsin, starting the night shift at eight dollars an hour plus university benefits. Even though the evening corridors were empty and echoing, the family's monthly income doubled. Living frugally, Tenzin and Migmar contributed, as did most other Tibetan Americans in town, toward additions and upkeep at Deer Park Buddhist Temple and support of political prisoners in Tibet. They sent money to India to help Migmar's family start a sweater-selling business.

"They think we're rich." Tenzin complained mildly, shaking her head. "They have no idea how hard we work."

Tenzin was working nearly ninety hours a week. With Migmar matching her hours and soon the older children holding weekend part-time jobs, the family worked the equivalent of six full-time jobs at nine dollars an hour, comparable to one professional making fifty-four dollars an hour, or more than one hundred thousand dollars a year. By September 2000, Tenzin made a down payment on a split-level, four-bedroom house in the middle of Madison. She became indignant over how much interest she would pay over thirty years, so she halved her mortgage to fifteen years and doubled her monthly payments to the bank.

Tenzin worked with purpose, rarely flagging, and yet she was nostalgic for the casual pace of work back in India.

"In India we were outdoors," she told me. "There were animals to feed, corn to plant, then the harvest, when we worked hard, long hours. But it was our pace. When harvest [was] finished, we were [able to] work easy again.

"Here, there's lots of pressure all year. Hours are late. I worry about layoffs. In India I was young, and I had lots of energy. Now I'm getting slow. My feet burn. Too much bending. Too many toilets. Lifting beds all day. Back aching." She pointed to her lower back, then her neck, wrists, forearms, knees, and arches, all points where her arthritis throbbed.

Working three to four simultaneous jobs had costs beyond exhaustion and physical wear and tear. Little time was left for her children and none for English classes or to start progress toward a GED. She never mentioned her dream to take her family to Wisconsin Dells, much less the Grand Canyon.

~

At school, the children's ESL teachers became my new heroines. At home, all four of the teens spoke of "Mrs. Garcia" and "Mrs. Kaplan" so often that Migmar, Tenzin, and I felt that we knew them. Close in age and grade level, sometimes two or even three of the older kids would be in the same class, learning alongside students who spoke different languages at different proficiency levels, all struggling to learn English. Their two ESL teachers, Judith Garcia Landsman and Catherine Kaplan, went out of their way to correctly pronounce and spell all their students' names and build lessons around the students' various ethnicities, religions, and the often-broiling political issues in their home countries. From what she had learned at school, Lhadon informed me that "American" holidays included the Mexican Day of the Dead, Chinese New Year, and Ramadan.

～

During her first year in Madison, one of Lhadon's classmates was an eighth grader who had moved to the city for the year from the People's Republic of China. She went by the Americanized name of Donna. "Lhadon and Donna glared at one another when they met," Mrs. Garcia told me later. "I remember Donna running to me one day in tears, saying, 'Lhadon is mean to me.'"

By the end of the school year, the girls were close friends. At one of the school's international days, where students learn about each other's heritage, Lhadon and Donna decided to switch and wear one another's traditional costumes. "Teaching doesn't get better than this," Mrs. Garcia recalled. "Two girls who can become friends, when their governments could not."

Not all teachers were trained to teach ELL students, however. In the so-called regular classrooms, students from vastly different backgrounds sat side by side, listening as teachers tried to explain the complexities of their given subjects, often without training in cultural sensitivity or communication techniques effective with ESL students. When Lhadon entered eighth grade near the end of the school year, her social studies class had been studying the US Civil War. The first chapter Lhadon tackled was titled "Reconstruction." At the end of that school year, I came across her final social studies exam in a pile of crumpled school papers in her bedroom. The teacher had given an open-ended prompt: "Choose one person who lived during the time of the Civil War. Write about his/her life, and tell how the Civil War affected him/her."

Lhadon had left the answer space blank, except for writing a question in return, "What is Civil War?"

In answer to her scrawled question on the sheet, the teacher had written, "I am going to cry."

"Lhadon," I explained, too late to make a difference in her grade, "a civil war is when people in the same country fight one another. Like in India, when the Hindus and the Muslims fought one another, and Pakistan was separated from India."

"Oh!" she said, her eyes flying open in surprise. Suddenly she was interested. "Did that happen here?" I pictured the teacher, talking every day, unaware that the central lesson, what was a civil war, was flying over the head of the quiet girl at the back of the room.

Students like Namgyal, Lhadon, Tamdin, and Thardoe, often fluent in two or three home languages, slipped through the day, counting the hours until their ESL class. There, somehow, they and their classmates could suddenly understand the teacher's clear explanations and careful English.

As powerful as ESL instruction was, however, it masked other needs students might have. By the end of high school, I suspected at least one of the four had dyslexia, something that could and should have been tested and addressed much earlier.

Because they were essentially nonreaders in their own Tibetan language, in which they had only a few years of instruction, and nonreaders in Hindi, which they had barely had an opportunity to study in India, the children also became essentially nonreaders in English. Part of this was cultural. In old Tibet, monks had comprised the literary class, mastering sutras, scriptures, prayers, and religious treatises during long years of study. Common people, the herders and farmers, had a rich oral tradition of folktales, folk songs, riddles, proverbs, tongue twisters, chants, and wedding and funeral speeches, but few academic opportunities. Only children of wealthy landowners went to school. At home in Madison, Migmar and Tenzin seldom read books, magazines, or newspapers for pleasure, whether English, Hindi, or Tibetan. The children followed suit. By the time they graduated from high school, I counted that among the four of them, they had read a total of six books "for pleasure." In fairness, I admit that I, who studied French for four years, have never chosen to read a book in French for pleasure, and do not subscribe to foreign-language newspapers or magazines either.

When there was a reason to read, however, the children could work very hard. A high school social studies teacher, collaborating with the ESL staff, challenged Namgyal and Tamdin to defend their oft-stated belief that Tibetans deserved their country back from China. The teacher observed the guys wearing their Free Tibet T-shirts, day after day.

"Is it really possible to free Tibet?" he asked them, playing devil's advocate. "Isn't that an unrealistic dream? Isn't it too late? And what is Tibetan Buddhism, anyway?"

The teacher's challenge sent both boys running to school library computers. They each turned in a thirty-page paper, explaining the seven symbols of Tibetan Buddhism, the Tibetan Book of the Dead, and the written Tibetan script. Actually, these were topics the boys themselves knew little about, and they copied and pasted sections directly from Wikipedia. The jumble of paragraphs and topics showed they understood little about how to organize a research paper. I wasn't sure they could even read what they had copied, but I was amazed by the quantity of work and their passion and interest. Too many hours of school went by, however, without such sparks that ignited connections between present and past, between school and real life.

～

Migmar and Tenzin's lack of sleep increasingly concerned me.

"Tenzin," I asked one day, "how many hours of sleep do you get?"

"I don't know," she said, shrugging. "We take a nap after lunch when we come home from Kennedy Manor. Then we wake up at 4:30 in the afternoon to get ready to work at the university."

"And then what?" I probed.

"We get home, watch TV to relax, then go to sleep about 2 a.m. We get up 6 a.m."

I counted on my fingers. "That's only six hours total, sometimes five."

Week in and week out, Tenzin and Migmar slept in two intervals, an afternoon nap between jobs, then four hours of sleep when they returned home in the dead of night. Hardly a minute was left over; errands, socializing, watching TV, and cooking got shoved into the weekends. I tried not to think about sleep deprivation data—increased accidents, stress, obesity, blood pressure, heart attacks, strokes. Finally, Tenzin quit her weekend jobs. I took care not to telephone before ten o'clock on Saturday and Sunday mornings so she could catch up on sleep.

During the week, her night-shift hours were long and lonely. She looked forward to the 9 p.m. break, when workers met, ate a meal, and socialized. Tenzin called these coworkers her second family.

"One guy is lazy," she told me. "He borrowed my broom, didn't return it. Borrowed my pail, didn't return. I went up to his floor and yelled at him, 'You got to be responsible! We are second family. You got to respect me, return my stuff.'

"'I don't care,' he told me."

Her temper flared, and she yelled back at him, "I'm your family! You gotta care!"

Her university colleagues were family; her Kennedy Manor residents were family; I was family. From a family-strong culture, Tenzin's embrace encompassed many. I wished I could send her to serve at the United Nations to yell at those world leaders, "You gotta care!"

~

Migmar's minimal English surged dramatically during two years when an hour of English instruction was offered twice a week from 11 p.m. to midnight at the university for interested cleaning crew members.

"Who is teaching you English in the middle of the night?" I asked, suspecting that only a woman would take such a job.

"Shoko," Migmar replied.

Of course, I thought, recognizing a Japanese name—not only a woman, but a woman from another country. Even when the university ceased giving midnight English lessons, due to budget cuts, Shoko remained a treasured family friend. Migmar went back to relying on his wife and children for translations, but I had glimpsed that quick and eager learner who had, decades ago, wished fervently for more schooling.

~

In the years following the family's reunion in Madison, I spent a lot of time at their house, located on a busy boulevard. Because Tenzin and Migmar were often at work, I would ring the doorbell at the end of my own workday and barge in as soon as one of them unlocked the door.

"Turn off the TV," I would say, bossy and parent-like, not realizing what a superb teacher a television could be for students learning English. All four children would groan, while one would head to the kitchen to boil Tibetan-style sugar tea or butter tea for me.

"Go outside and play," I would encourage them. "Get some fresh air." "Read a book." Or, "Let's go to the library."

I had many ideas, not all laudable. With a stop at McDonald's one day early on, I introduced them to the combined pleasures of grease, salt, and a moving vehicle. The teenaged cashier handed five small packets of French fries through the drive-up window. Namgyal helped me pass them back. The car became quiet, just the repeated crackle of ketchup packets being ripped open. Another evening, after a tutoring session, I took them to Pizza Hut for their first pepperoni pizza. When the pizza arrived, none of them moved to eat it. They snickered. Eight eyes studied me as I unwrapped my silverware from its tightly rolled napkin, reached for a sloppy slice, slid it onto my plate, then picked up my fork. They each followed suit, giggling at one another's copycat gestures. Soon I was laughing too, witness to another cultural mundanity unraveled, silverware. Quickly I realized that since they were used to eating with their hands at home, we may as well eat pizza this way too, and soon we were all munching our pizza slices and licking our fingers, American style, Tibetan style, whichever, still laughing.

◆

Namgyal, Lhadon, Tamdin, and Thardoe quickly picked up nuances of social class. Because of their parents' initial minimum-wage incomes, all four kids qualified for the public school sub-sidized meal program. Tamdin and Lhadon were delighted to discover that in addition to the free lunch, the middle school also offered free breakfast. For the first three days, they happily went to school forty-five minutes early, exclaiming over both white and chocolate milk, cereal in small boxes, white and brown-colored bread slices, and generous fruit servings that were put out for the students. But by Thursday, they had picked up on the stigma associated with such programs and refused to participate. "It's just for poor kids," Lhadon informed me.

Day after day, Migmar offered to pack Indian curries and Tibetan rice dishes for the kids' lunches. "Not today," they would mumble to him. Sometimes they went through the cafeteria line, embarrassed when the woman at the cash register took an extra minute to punch a separate "Free Lunch" card for them. In the cafeteria, overwhelmed at the gaggles of chattering kids they didn't know, they would carry their trays to eat in the ESL classroom with friends. By high school, not unlike other teens, they often skipped lunch entirely. Like other parents, I would deposit money to their lunch cards, unaware.

～

As the oldest, Namgyal became the pioneer, the first to brave a high school with an enrollment in the hundreds. By that time he had already heard the word "bully" and at school witnessed instances of kids, often students of color, often short or slender, not unlike him, getting pushed around or beaten up. He decided that looking fierce and tough, staring straight ahead, and speaking to no one as he changed classes was the way to stay unnoticed. By his second year, he had made friends with Hmong American and Cambodian American guys in his ESL classes. Together they could saunter their way down the halls, joking with one another. No one messed with them.

～

Parenting is a maddening learning process, I realized, as I attempted to pitch in on this monumental task. How does one deal with teens who don't want to go anywhere or do anything? What is the balance between respecting a young man's shyness and self-consciousness and forcing him to try new things? Tamdin's recalcitrance infuriated and mystified me.

On one occasion, two of the brothers hopped into my car. I

cannot remember why Lhadon was not with us, but I had promised the three brothers a spring break camping trip in Door
County, Wisconsin's thumb-shaped peninsula that juts between
the waters of Green Bay and Lake Michigan.

"Where's Tamdin?" I asked.

"He's not going," Namgyal replied.

I left the two sitting in the car and stomped into the house.
Tamdin was sprawled on the sofa, playing a video game. I
cajoled: Door County is beautiful. We'll cook out on a grill and
sleep in a tent. How can he know he doesn't want to go? He
shook his head no and pulled sofa pillows on top of himself as
I became more agitated. Finally, I pulled him off the sofa,
dragged him across the carpet, then over the lawn, smearing
grass stains onto his Free Tibet T-shirt, right to the car.

"Get in!" I demanded, not caring if any neighbor might
witness what was far from my finest moment.

I wheeled around and pointed at the two waiting brothers.
"You, find his backpack and his jacket. You, get his shoes and
his swim trunks." I sat fuming in the driver's seat with the child
lock button on, preventing Tamdin's escape. He simmered in a
silent pout for the entire five hours it took us to get to our destination, punishing my conversation attempts with scowls. After
we arrived, he resumed being his merry, mischievous self, and
I sighed with relief, glad that I, a woman without children, had
only occasionally to deal with the ferocities of teen defiance.

By the time the boys had hiked in three state parks, explored
lighthouses, skipped stones, hot-tubbed, picnicked, sampled
the meatballs in Al Johnson's Swedish Restaurant, climbed
trees, had sword fights with sticks, and wrestled and chased
one another all through Door County, the excursion seemed
like a success.

Later in college and graduate school, Tamdin wrote eloquently about his lack of self-confidence and acute self-

consciousness following the upheaval of leaving his home culture. I wished instead of losing my temper on occasion, I had had the presence of mind to talk to him more calmly about the necessity of trusting his abilities and needing to make mistakes along the way, to learn new things. But I, too, was learning to trust my instincts and forgive myself for my own mistakes.

꙳

Not just Tamdin but also Migmar and Tenzin suffered from my know-it-all approach to things involving the children.

One afternoon, looking through a stack of mail that Tenzin asked me to check for "anything important," I happened upon a postcard that requested her to make an appointment with one of the children's teachers.

"Tenzin," I asked, "do you know that employers are required to give you time off to attend parent-teacher conferences?"

"They won't pay me if I leave in the middle of the day," she objected.

"True," I agreed. "It would be time without pay. But you have the right to ask for that time off."

Both she and her employers were surprised to learn this. The many resulting back-and-forth exchanges among me, Tenzin, her supervisors, and the teachers at school soon felt like a waste of time. Tenzin gave up. I gave up, too. Migmar and Tenzin entered their children's schools rarely, embarrassed that they had only completed fifth and sixth grades, feeling awkward not to know the protocol for interacting with their kids' teachers. I enjoyed spending time with the children and serving as the family's school liaison. I didn't realize the greater impact I might have had by empowering Tenzin and Migmar to study English and complete their GEDs, or by modeling ways they could have encouraged their children to do homework. I should have found time and reason to accompany them into the children's schools. The teachers, too, missed an opportunity to meet inspiring, hardworking immigrant parents.

While I felt the advantages of being in this family's life, I seldom considered the negative aspects, for them, of having me around. In retrospect, I could have done much more to share skills with them to navigate their children's new world. I skimmed a lot of cream.

~

For me, the cherry atop the cream was sharing my love of travel. After decades of journeying solo, I delighted in having fun, funny travel companions. When I needed to visit my elderly Aunt Betty and sister Susan in Denver in 2001, all three boys journeyed with me across the Plains states by Amtrak. We shared a sleeper car, and they adored the double bunk bed set-up—so much so, they didn't want to leave it. I hadn't expected to have a hard time coaxing them to the dome car to get 180-degree views of the fields, cities, and rivers rushing by.

I think it was shy Tamdin who convinced the other two to stay put. Even the conductor was soon in on the game, winking at the teens and bringing them hamburgers so they wouldn't have to go with me to the dining car. I ate alone.

Back at home after a week in Denver, all three of them interrupted one another and howled with laughter as they told their parents about the Mile High City's skyscrapers, Natural History Museum, and Tibetan artifacts at the public library. They agreed on the highlights: the train ride, hiking in the Rocky Mountains, and two nights all by themselves in a posh suite in Burnsley Hotel, an inspired gift from my sister Susan.

Lhadon accompanied me on one of my trips to visit my Oklahoma family, where she bonded with my niece Carol, close in age. Another time, she and one of her friends accompanied me to New York City, where they seemed simultaneously grown up and impressionable.

Only Namgyal didn't instantly pick up the travel bug. After he had to miss a trip to Portland, Oregon, when the three other kids shared Thanksgiving with my brother David and sister Susan, I took only him with me to a Uraneck summer family reunion at Lake Tahoe, Nevada. I purchased two super-cheap tickets on Priceline. Perhaps it was the wrong event—too many old people, too many little kids, no siblings. And we had to change flights multiple times—in Denver and Salt Lake City to get there, then in San Francisco and St. Louis on the return trip. What a great way to see America, I reasoned, but it was also a head-swimming itinerary. At an airport bookstore, I purchased a basketball magazine, after which it seemed like his head never came out of it.

"Look! Look! Namgyal!" I tried to get his attention on one flight. "There's the Golden Gate Bridge right out the window." I had let him have my window seat. He didn't glance up.

"I don't want to see it," he said.

Ruefully, he said, years later, "I didn't know American history or geography. I'd like to do that trip again."

It was no matter—even if they had different ways of perceiving it, they were seeing something of the America I loved.

～

One Saturday, as I sat in their living room drinking sugar tea and milk, freshly boiled on the stove, Tenzin said, just in passing, "I tell my kids, Madeline is getting older. When she's old, you take care of her. Don't worry, Madeline, they'll be there for you."

I glanced at Lhadon, who was leafing through a magazine. Her expression was unreadable. A promise to care for a nonrelated elder was a lot to elicit from a teen. Even my own siblings and nieces made no such offers. I had always assumed I would be responsible for finding my own caretakers and residency in old age. I had never imagined, and wasn't sure I would ever count on, the kids in this family becoming responsible for my personal care. From that moment on, however, I began suspecting that our involvement in each other's lives was a two-way street.

~

Sometime in the family's second year in Madison, I realized theirs was one of the few homes in the world where I felt completely comfortable. Odors of curries and peppery sauces infused the walls and carpets. The TV was always on. There were no expectations of me: I could stop by for ten minutes or stay the whole day. I could take a nap on one of the soft leather sofas if I was sleepy. Tenzin and Migmar had created a warm nest, and the children felt secure in its protective safety. In that house they could be themselves, speak Tibetan, joke around, play video games, or watch Hindi DVDs rented from the Indian grocery store. I, too, could stretch out, drink my tea, and chat with whomever was in the room—people who every day seemed more like my own family, only more respectful, more fascinating—people who seemed to accept me in their intimate space.

I fell increasingly in love with each of the children. They were very different from one another, but each brimmed with talent, curiosity, and warmth. Namgyal was responsible and decisive, the first to volunteer for a task and the first to finish. Lhadon, a new brand of American feminist, was simultaneously strong and tender. Tamdin, if stubborn, was thoughtful and observant. His stories captured cultural differences and put a finger on the oddities of personalities. Easygoing Thardoe, the youngest, often made everyone laugh. He could diffuse tempers before they erupted, and when in a group, he often looked around to make sure everyone was served and included.

Somehow, I had lucked into four children not mine, each one enriching my life and making me acutely aware of my every value, my every hypocrisy, and my need to offer pieces of my underused heart.

CHAPTER 6

Becoming American

I'm interested in people who find themselves in places, either of their own choosing or not, and who are forced to decide how best to live there. That feeling of both citizen and exile, of always being an expatriate—and all the attendant problems and complications and delight.
—Chang Rae Lee, South Korean novelist

After the arrival of so many families, the Tibetan American community in Madison turned its concern to the cultural and historical education of its children. Initially, on Tuesday and Thursday nights, a University of Wisconsin chapter of Students for a Free Tibet offered tutoring sessions in space lent by a local church. It was a mutual admiration society: the younger newcomers were in awe of the hip, easygoing college students, who in turn were delighted to know dozens of energetic, engaging "real" Tibetan youngsters.

High school students took the one-on-one tutoring sessions seriously, but the younger kids, who often had no homework assigned by their teachers at school, were giggly and rambunctious. Whether older or younger, all the kids seemed to love getting to know Tibetan-speaking peers from other Madison schools, mostly youth they had never met back in their Indian or Nepali settlements. Though I couldn't understand or distinguish between them, different Tibetan and Nepali dialects danced through the halls and study rooms.

In just one year, many of the cultural practices the children brought with them had been replaced by American ones. Like other adolescents, they wandered in shopping malls, yearned to buy cool-looking clothes, ate junk food, imbibed Coca-Cola, and seemed increasingly self-conscious about being out in public with their parents. In their first days here, the four siblings had been happy to sit in their living room and draw sophisticated landscapes and portraits with crayons. A new TV and an Xbox for video games put an end to this.

During their first month in the United States, the family went on walks together at sunset, like they had in India. There, parents and children strolled together in the early evenings down roads, across little bridges, and past shops or market stands with sellers of peanuts and trinkets, greeting other families as they passed. In Madison, they soon ceased their sunset walks.

"No one else is walking," Tenzin explained.

The family retreated indoors, with a parade of television channels replacing the interactive parade through neighborhoods.

～

"We never had a toy," Lhadon said matter-of-factly.

"Any toy?" I asked, disbelieving. "Not a doll, a jump rope, jacks, anything?"

"Nope," she said.

"Nope," echoed Thardoe.

The topic had come up because Lhadon had been assigned to write a story for her eighth-grade English class, "My Favorite Toy." She wrote about a Barbie doll that broke.

"But, Lhadon," I said, "this is not true. You told me you never had any toys in India."

She ripped the draft into pieces and threw it on the floor. "I don't want to write!"

"Lhadon, you have to write it again. I'll sit with you. Go get your backpack and find a pencil."

Sulkily, she started again with a blank sheet of paper. By the end of an hour, with some coaching, Lhadon had written a charming story about how thrilled she had been, in India, when the older girls finally let her play hop scotch with them. I never saw her grade. I hoped the teacher had recognized it as an authentic story.

For Thardoe's twelfth birthday, I gave him a twenty-five-dollar gift certificate to Toys R Us.

"You can buy anything except a video game," I told him. Thardoe spent a full hour walking up and down the aisles. Finally he settled on a barnyard animal set—a cow, horse, chicken, goat, and sheep. I felt a pang—this boy so tall and mature-looking, already sprouting facial hair, was happy with this simple toy set, one that might delight a three-year-old. The barnyard animals lined up atop the TV set for many years, content to watch Bollywood videos with the family.

∼

With three athletic boys who had played hours of European football in India and who loved watching World Cup Soccer, I thought soccer would be the perfect outlet for their long summer days, since school was out and their parents worked. I looked forward to enrolling them on soccer teams and in summer soccer camps.

"We can all be on the same team!" the boys exclaimed, imagining foiling the other players with the combined moves they had practiced, barefoot, on their settlement green.

Soccer teams in the United States, however, are strictly

governed by birth dates, and the boys learned they could play only if they played on three different teams. In addition, I had missed the all-important deadlines for team registration. The boys were told they could not start midseason. That first summer, we scored zero.

One afternoon my friend Willi, who was a youth soccer coach, let all three of them suit up in red jerseys, baggy, black shorts, red socks, and cleats to join his team for a friendly scrimmage. The boys were elated, even if this was just a one-time opportunity.

Willi immediately started yelling at them.

"Move the ball! Pass! Pass!"

The boys were like puppies, hogging the ball, showing off with intricate twirls and spins, and if they passed, it was only to one another, as they had done in India. In the United States, soccer was more linear, directional, and score-oriented. Points counted, and a team won or lost. Here, soccer was not an informal game of neighborhood fun; it was a miniature, high-stakes athletic competition in which parents lined up to encourage and yell from the sidelines.

All three boys were quiet on the way home.

By the next summer, I realized that if I were to get all three boys to early evening soccer practices at three different times, on three different sides of town, I would have to quit my day job. How did other parents do it?

"We carpool," a nice mom explained. I called people I didn't know, asking if they could pick up Thardoe, or take him to weekend games, which often involved four hours of round-trip travel. Though these families all seemed to live on the West Side of Madison, and Thardoe lived on the East Side, they were willing and generous to make an extra detour.

"He's a go-getter!" the parents would tell me later, as Thardoe hopped out of a car. All the parents seemed to know his name. "Thardoe! Thardoe!" they chanted from the sidelines. His grace and natural athleticism were obvious.

But Thardoe mentioned that the games were "too far" and that he didn't understand what people were saying in the car during the long trips there and back. He missed playing with his brothers, whom I hadn't managed to put on teams yet. Soccer seemed to involve more time, travel, and networking than I or the boys' parents could manage.

It was a joyous day, therefore, when the Wisconsin Tibetan Association founded its own soccer team, the Yak Boys. Brothers could be on the same team, and the fathers had a team as well. Tibetans in Madison arranged to play teams from other Tibetan American communities as far away as Minneapolis and Chicago, and even New York City. The uniforms blazed with the sun design of Tibet's flag. Sometimes the kids encountered classmates from their former settlement. The Madison Yak Boys carried home the league trophy for the Midwest Pawo Thupten Ngodup Soccer Championship in 2002 and for six straight years, from 2005 to 2010.

↪

As family members, all the children were expected to help their parents, but the work was a long way from the "real work" they had done in India.

"In India we picked up cow manure and made it into patties for the stove." Lhadon fell over on the living room carpet, laughing, as she told me this, and her brothers Namgyal and Tamdin hooted uproariously as well. What would their Madison classmates say to this?

I frequently argued with Tenzin about how Lhadon, as a girl, was expected to be at home at all times. Lhadon was supposed to vacuum, clean both bathrooms, help her father cook breakfast and her mother cook supper, and do the dishes at every meal. The three boys, meanwhile, watched TV in the living room or wrestled and played video games in their bedrooms. Lhadon incurred Tenzin's wrath by meeting high school friends at the mall to chat and try on clothes.

"She needs friends her age," I argued. But Tenzin ignored my interventions. She spoke directly to Lhadon.

"You waste money."

"You talk on the phone too much."

"Your friends are no good."

Her father and brothers harangued her as well. One day as I was pulling into the driveway, I met Lhadon on her way out, slamming the door and yelling to no one in particular, "I hate my life!"

I intercepted her, concerned. "Is it because kids at school are giving you a hard time?"

"No, I hate being in this family!" she said. It seemed an answer any US teenager might give in a moment of rage. Yet I saw her dilemma: Her family wanted her to be a modest, quiet, obedient daughter, as she would be expected to be back in the Tibetan community in India. Lhadon had instead grown up here to be a funny and generous young woman with opinions and preferences that reflected those of teens in Madison.

It was when I looked at Lhadon—who wanted, as much as any female her age, to be pretty, popular, and fashionable, while her mother scrubbed the floors in Madison—that I most felt the divisions of age, class, and ethnicity that separated me from the family. On one side were hardworking women such as Tenzin who had had to drop out of school early, caught in an inequitable cycle of low-wage jobs; on the other, my friends and I, affluent, college-educated, living amidst a wealth of opportunities and networks. Caught in the middle was Lhadon, a first-generation immigrant daughter negotiating what it meant to be female in a city whose mores were feminist and permissive.

One day, Lhadon returned from a shopping trip, her arms laden with packages, probably new clothes. The money she had spent was from her own wages from her part-time job.

"You do not respect me," Tenzin hissed at her daughter, disapproving probably of both the purchases and the mall destination. "You do not respect this family."

Lhadon's eyes filled with tears, and she stomped upstairs and slammed her bedroom door. In a culture grounded on respect and family ties, those were hurtful words.

When Migmar and Tenzin lived in India and envisioned their lives in America, they probably assumed that childrearing would transfer easily from one country to the next. In their sunny settlement in Bylakuppe, children ran here and there on errands, shared housework, and played outdoors in the open spaces. In Madison, the children lived indoors. Regardless of the weather outside, they watched TV and teased one another; the boys played endless hours of *Mortal Combat* or wrestled on the carpet while Lhadon cooked in the kitchen. The yelling that goes on among parents and children was there, but soon after arriving in the United States, the children told their parents, in all seriousness, something they had heard at school.

"You can't hit us. If you hit us, we will call 911. The cops will come and put you in jail."

"Is this true?" Tibetan parents asked one another at the Wisconsin Tibetan Association meetings at the University Heights community center.

"It must be true," other parents confirmed. "Our children told us the same thing."

"How on earth will we get our kids to obey?" the parents asked.

I wondered if Migmar and Tenzin saw it as all or nothing—if they couldn't use the discipline they were used to, how could they discipline them at all? They looked askance at the adolescents they saw on Madison streets: girls unaccompanied by parents or brothers, heads bare of scarves, with tight pants and tanned bellies showing off pierced navels. They heard from their children that students in high school smoked cigarettes, took drugs at parties, had sex, got pregnant, and even had abortions. Just what did "being American" mean? As I observed them with their peers, I saw no indication they might fling themselves off a social precipice into a canyon of sex and drugs. Still, Migmar and Tenzin seemed adrift. It was easier to exchange a *chupa* for a blue jean jacket than it was to trade one's way of parenting to find a new one that fit.

~

My Tibetan American family and I fluctuated between being insiders and outsiders within one another's communities. Either I was an outsider at Tibetan American events, or the children and their parents were outsiders at the casual, university-connected or Folklore Village events to which I took them.

At family gatherings and big events, my Tibetan family and other Tibetan Americans continued speaking in Tibetan when I sat down beside them.

"How are you?" they would ask, turning to address me in English.

Once I answered, they would resume talking in Tibetan, sometimes explaining who I was and how we had met, seemingly unaware that I was excluded, even though I was sitting right there, often the subject of their very conversations. I was sure my rapid-fire, slang-filled English, with topics of interest to me and my friends, was equally exclusionary.

One day, two years after their arrival, Lhadon asked me, "How do you make friends with white people?"

She was in tenth grade. I pictured her in the cavernous halls of the high school and answered her question with another. "What do you do between classes?"

"I talk with my friends," she said.

I imagined a group of Tibetan American teens congregated together and laughing. "What language do you speak with them?" I asked, already suspecting one problem.

"Tibetan," she confirmed.

At least part of the solution seemed obvious to me. "Try speaking some English in the hall," I suggested. After two more years, Lhadon graduated. Her friends—smart, sensible, sophisticated, some college-bound, some not—continued to be mostly of Tibetan ethnicity.

Sometimes the boys and I went jogging together. Faster than me, they ran through the neighborhoods, past shady mansions with three-car garages and professionally landscaped lawns. Suddenly a patrol car would be following them. What could it mean that brown-skinned boys were running through an affluent neighborhood? I would catch up with them, gasping for breath, and the patrol car would speed off, suddenly disinterested.

Other times, we would walk into a gas station, the three tall brothers preceding me. The clerk would look up, panic on his face, eyeing his telephone. As I joined them a moment later, usually saying something to let the clerk know we were together, he would visibly relax. Class, race, ethnicity: I began to experience Madison on multiple levels, one that was kind and inclusive, another that was meaner or more exclusive; one that welcomed diversity, another that regarded brown-skinned people with suspicion or fear, welcoming people of color only at certain events, preferably in costume and in small numbers.

~

"My own children do not love me," Tenzin murmured sadly one day. "They love Migmar."

When she had flown from India to the United States, Tenzin had left her young children in Migmar's care. The boys remained in the settlement with Migmar and their grandmother, or Momo, as they called Tenzin's mother. As a farmer, Migmar found many hours to play with them, cook for them, and go with them to holiday events at the community center. He told them old Tibetan stories, ones he had heard during his own childhood, in the evenings. Twice a year, he accompanied small Lhadon on the train to Bangalore, then Chennai, where, together with many other Tibetan refugee girls, she attended a Catholic boarding school, her tuition paid by an aunt.

Pah-lak, the Tibetan word for "father," rippled through the day. The teens' adoration for their father was palpable, especially the boys'. They switched from English to Tibetan if they noticed him excluded from conversations. They pulled him into minor daily decisions and joked with him.

"What's Migmar saying?" I asked one day, as Migmar shouted animatedly during a Green Bay Packers football game on TV.

Thardoe translated. "He said that Aaron Rodgers threw to the wrong guy. He said Aaron Rodgers can't run fast enough."

"Oh," I replied, disappointed. In the midst of spoken Tibetan, I often assumed I was missing gems of Buddhist wisdom. Apparently guy talk around the world, in front of a TV set, shared a narrower focus.

When I consulted Migmar about something, he would wave me away. "Ask Tenzin Kalsang. She knows." He trusted Tenzin to pay the bills, call appliance repairmen, and schedule time with friends and family. His respect for her was solid. The children loved her but expressed it differently, with courtesy, understanding, and obedience. Except for Tamdin, the boys learned to cook a little; Lhadon not only fixed meals for her parents but packed them lunches for their next day of work. She and her brothers prepared Tenzin's favorite south Indian dishes for her birthday. They cleaned their rooms and turned off lights each time they exited a room, and Lhadon kept the house shining, all things to show their mom, or Ama-lak as they called her, that they loved her. She was their taskmaster, like many moms the world over, offering advice and admonishments freely, and needing an occasional "Thanks, Mom."

~

On the Bylakuppe settlement, Migmar and Tenzin got places by walking, biking, driving a tractor, or hopping into a crowded van or rickety bus. In Wisconsin, adults needed a car and a driver's license. I had taught many people to drive so didn't hesitate to get Tenzin and Migmar on the road.

"Look left and right when you go past a street, Migmar! Just little looks—like this, eyes here, eyes there." I pointed to my eyes, glancing right and left. Migmar chuckled and continued to look only straight ahead as he plowed through residential intersections.

When he wanted to change lanes, he signaled, then slid over gracefully.

"No! Migmar, you have to look before you change lanes!" My voice rose several octaves, as the driver behind us veered, honked, then gunned past with an extended middle finger. Migmar didn't notice because he was staring straight ahead. His hands grasped the wheel, his arms as stiff as ramrods, and his speed never varied. He failed his first and second driver's license exams.

Tenzin was a timid learner. "I can't do it," she said, laughing apologetically.

"Just drive," I commanded humorlessly, determined to convey that quitting or failing were not options. My car was an automatic. She put her foot on the accelerator, and the car inched forward in the empty church parking lot. She burst out laughing with surprise and took her foot off the accelerator, but the car kept slowly rolling forward.

"Brake," I reminded her, as the car followed a slight dip in the pavement. "Stop the car. Put your foot on the other pedal. Brake!"

The last imperative was a shout as the car approached boulders that edged the lot. She slammed on the brakes. Although seat-belted in for this creep around the parking lot, our bodies jerked toward the windshield.

"Try again," I sighed, trying to regain my inner monk. "Next time, brake gently."

Tenzin also failed her first two attempts at the driving exam. By her second attempt, I knew the names of the examiners, and they knew ours.

Without mentioning it to me, Tenzin and Migmar took on teaching themselves, late at night after work, and they might have passed the third time had they not made the mistake of driving themselves to the license test. The examiner discovered that neither had a driver's license and sent them home. The boys, who had already passed their own tests with ease, took over their parents' lessons, explaining things gently and in Tibetan, more conscious than I of what might be difficult for them.

Their fourth attempt spelled success. Migmar immediately purchased a used Mercury station wagon, the color of eggplant, big enough to carry everyone. The boys and Lhadon bought cars too. Tenzin announced she never would drive again. She managed just fine, with an abundance of drivers available and a garage and driveway filled with cars, just like the neighbors.

⁓

"Let's go! Let's go!" I shouted enthusiastically on a morning in 1999, herding the seven of us into our two cars for a drive to the federal building in downtown Madison. "Let's not be late. How often do you get to become an American citizen?"

I am a child of the 1960s Vietnam-era protests and am often critical of US foreign policy. Yet I looked at the red, white, and blue flag in the large chamber that day and felt immense pride to be an American. Tenzin was about to participate in one of the country's oldest, most venerable ceremonies: to become a naturalized US citizen.

Tenzin was dressed in new blue jeans, a blue jean jacket, and a corsage I had given her. She stood among about fifty others: women in long Somali dresses, short Latino men in khaki jackets, elderly white-haired men in suits, maybe from Eastern Europe or former Soviet countries. I had pulled the children out of three different schools for the day. We were crammed in the back of the room, watching as Tenzin raised her right hand and repeated the rather severe oath, phrase by phrase: "I hereby declare, on oath, that I absolutely and entirely renounce and abjure all allegiance and fidelity to any foreign prince, potentate, State, or sovereignty . . ."

We celebrated her special day with lunch at an Indian restaurant, where we sat at a round table as a waiter brought dish after dish. I saw other customers sneaking glances in our direction. We were a magnetic, merry group. We wore our particular American-ness confidently—skipping school, eating our favorite Indian curries, and beaming at Tenzin, our newly American mom, wife, and friend.

～

Once Tenzin became a citizen, the three youngest children were eligible for a citizenship ceremony that the US Citizenship and Immigration Services (formerly INS) regularly scheduled in larger cities across the country. Namgyal, at nineteen years old, was too old to qualify and had to complete the adult requirements, but Lhadon and Tamdin, and later Thardoe, all took their citizenship pledge in a federal courthouse in Milwaukee.

Again, I pulled all four kids out of school, and Migmar and Tenzin took the day off work. We fairly bounced with anticipation as we drove ninety minutes to Milwaukee, past dairy farms and forested drumlins.

The courthouse room was crowded with kids of many heights, hair lengths, and skin colors. "Lots of different country kids," whispered Thardoe, his eyes big. They all sported neon-colored Nikes or blue jeans and T-shirts, looking like ordinary elementary or high school students—no vestiges of heritage fabric, jewelry, or makeup among them.

After Tamdin and Lhadon's ceremony, we sat under gray skies on the banks of the Milwaukee River and had a picnic with all the foods we loved best, Tibetan *momo* (dumplings) with Migmar's tongue-curling hot sauce and fried samosas filled with spinach and cauliflower.

"My mom made a good choice," Thardoe reflected years later, about Tenzin's difficult decision to move her family to the United States. "In India, other relatives looked down on us because we were poor. Mom's relatives treated Dad poorly. They always asked him, 'How much do you make?' I knew Mom and Dad took out loans, then didn't have money to pay them back. They were always asking creditors to give us more time." He said this in a reflective tone. As they became older, I enjoyed hearing Thardoe and his siblings compare the pros and cons of their tricultural, trinational upbringing.

The paths to becoming an American were well trodden. While visiting my parents' home in Oklahoma that same year, I scrutinized my grandparents' yellowed citizenship paper in a frame that hung on the kitchen wall. Adam and Anna Juranek immigrated from Cieszyn, Poland, on the Czech-Polish border, in 1920. What had they felt on the day they were sworn in as US citizens? What had they lost and what had they gained? What had it meant for my grandparents to leave one home in a familiar land and follow unfamiliar paths to carve a home in another? The physical exhaustion and dangers of menial labor, the humiliation and frustrations of new parent-child relations, and the necessity of giving up personal dreams—these were building blocks of America's immigrant experience. I knew facts about my grandparents' lives. Now I could imagine their feelings. Despite the differences across time, ethnicity, race, and religion, I was pretty sure Tenzin and Migmar and Anna and Adam would have agreed about many things.

Migmar was the last of the six in his Wisconsin family to become a citizen. At his ceremony, I was curious about the oath that asked him to renounce allegiance to all other governments, knowing how fervently he dreamed that Tibet would once again be an independent country.

"Do you feel that you've lost your Tibetan citizenship, now that you're an American citizen?" I asked

He looked at me as if he was puzzled why I would ask such a naïve question.

"No paper," he said, which I took to mean that no paper could change who he was. "I'm Tibetan."

For him, citizenship was less about allegiance than about appreciation—appreciation for being together with his family, gratitude for opportunities for his children, freedom to travel back to India and to other countries, and the knowledge that he now lived in a country whose government would not throw him in jail for practicing his religion.

CHAPTER 7

⁓

Tenzin's Brilliant Idea

When I let go of what I am, I become what I might be.
—LAO TZU, ANCIENT CHINESE PHILOSOPHER

Once all four of Tenzin's children had graduated from high school, she decided to send her youngest, eighteen-year-old Thardoe, to India to learn *thangka*, a form of traditional Buddhist religious painting. *Thangka* paintings frequently depict a Buddha deity, or *mandala*. They adorn the walls of Buddhist temples and Buddhist family altars around the world, inspiring reverence and meditation. Nearly every Tibetan American family I visited owned at least one.

Thardoe had grown to be a gentle, good-natured young man and a gifted artist. He could easily draw portraits, animals, or landscapes, and he and his brother Tamdin filled notebooks with pencil sketches and watercolors, some of which hung on the family's walls.

Tenzin thought at least a year in India, possibly longer, would develop Thardoe's artistic talents and help him connect with his Tibetan heritage. Not only would Thardoe improve his drawing skills, but he would walk the cobblestone streets side by side with monks, with serious students of Tibetan studies, and with tourists who had journeyed far to experience the

Tibetan practices that were his birthright. What I didn't realize was that Tenzin had additional goals for Thardoe—and for me.

Thardoe liked the idea, not that he would have thought of refusing one of his mother's requests. In August of 2005, off he went, to live with family friends, artist Migmar Wangdu (whom I called Wangdu to avoid confusion with Tenzin's husband); his wife, Tsamchoe; and their two young children. The family lived in Dharamsala, the cool, mountainous city in northern India that had hosted Tibet's exiled government since 1960. While he was away, we exchanged a few e-mails. On November 7, 2005, he wrote:

> I live in Migmar [Wangdu]'s house who has wife and one beautiful daughter who is 6 months old and one crazy son who is 2 years old who I love to play kung fu with. My daily life is that I wake up in morning at 7:30 after doing morning chore. I go to school at 8:45 till 5:00. I drink tea and eat biscuit. Then I go play basketball with Migmar [Wangdu] down at the court. Right now I am doing slow on my studying with drawing gods but I am doing my best to improve.

Tibetans in India were in a heightened state of anticipation that year, as they prepared for a Kalachakra ceremony, the ancient initiation for serious practitioners of Buddhism, to be held in January 2006 in the town of Amaravati, in the southeastern Indian state of Andhra Pradesh. Once the site of a great temple that had long since fallen into ruin, Amaravati was known as the place where Buddha had given the very first Kalachakra. Not only would Thardoe be able to attend, but even Tenzin and Migmar had purchased plane tickets to Delhi to join him.

The Kalachakra ceremony is based on cycles of time, from the cycles of the planets to the cycles of one's own breathing. Every Tibetan Buddhist tries to attend at least one Kalachakra in her lifetime. The event begins as dozens of monks construct an intricate sand *mandala*; the initiation of devotees comes after days of preparation. Open to the public, the collective prayers, chants, and ceremonies are believed to increase the possibility for world peace, and to be a part of a Kalachakra is said to impart deep, spiritual knowledge. In Amaravati, more than one hundred thousand participants from seventy-one countries were pouring into town.

Thardoe wrote to me: "Mom told me to escort my Grandfather to Kalachakra. I am happy to do this. He is getting old, but he's a real interesting guy."

Traveling from northern to southern India, Thardoe journeyed by train seventeen hundred miles to meet his seventy-two-year-old grandfather, Tsewang Paldon. Startled, I realized this was the same man, Tenzin's father, who had been ill throughout her childhood. He had actually made it to old age. Thardoe's Aunt Dickey (Tenzin's sister) and her daughter Pema joined Thardoe as the train passed through Delhi. Once they helped the elderly man join their journey, the four traveled another eight hundred miles to Amaravati. Hundreds of fellow Indian Tibetans packed the train, talking animatedly, sharing lunches and tea.

Back in Wisconsin, amidst January preparations for her upcoming pilgrimage to Amaravati, Tenzin surprised me. "Madeline, you go to India, too," she declared. "Take Susan, your sister. You can visit all my relatives."

"Go with you to the Kalachakra?" I asked, not sure how well I, a Unitarian raised in the Bible Belt, would do if dropped into an intensive, thirteen-day religious ceremony.

"No, no! Kalachakra is this January. You go later. Thardoe's school finishes in August. Go then, and bring Thardoe home. Take Namgyal and Tamdin with you. They can show you around."

I was stunned. As I helped this family, I hadn't expected to gain anything more than their friendship. Now Tenzin had just opened a door to a wondrous labyrinth of people and places I had never dreamed of exploring. I had passed briefly through India in 1988, en route home from three years in Japan, and had visited Delhi, the Taj Mahal in Agra, and a Muslim host family in Lucknow, barely off the tourist track. To see India through the eyes of Thardoe and his brothers appealed enormously.

I had just applied to serve as a late-in-life Peace Corps volunteer, but I wouldn't start for eleven more months. This meant a trip to India in August was doable. As proposed by Tenzin, the four of us—Namgyal, Tamdin, my sister Susan, and I—would fly to Delhi, visit the family's relatives there, then travel north by bus to Dharamsala to meet Thardoe during his last days of *thangka* school. The five of us then would journey the full length of India by train, no small distance, to visit the family's former home in Bylakuppe, in southern India. My head was spinning. I suddenly realized I held a unique passport to culture, family heritage, and three important sites of the Tibetan diaspora.

~

Namgyal and Tamdin had huge grins as they anticipated our journey together. "Now, Madeline," said Namgyal expansively, "we will be *your* guides. We will teach you everything." They had left India as children; they would be returning as men, affluent, successful, and lucky in the eyes of their peers.

My sister Susan, who was living with me in those years, was less thrilled. She preferred me to be the family sojourner, while she remained ensconced in our cozy cottage on Madison's Lake Mendota to drink strong coffee, visit public libraries, and experience global complexities from the safe distance of my famously long emails.

"Look, I'm going to go into the Peace Corps after this," I wheedled. "We won't see each other for two whole years."

It was the persuading argument.

"I didn't sleep," she grumbled the next day. "I dread this trip already."

"But, Susan, why?"

"I'm just going so I can protect you. You're always so blasé about dangers."

"What dangers?"

"Like people who exploit tourists like you. Like disease. Like world crises that can happen."

Despite Susan's worries, August arrived, and our trip was on schedule. Namgyal and Tamdin would fly to Delhi first, and Susan and I would follow a week later. My colleagues, familiar with my work assignments that involved international travel, assumed I had long since mastered essentials such as vaccinations and visas. Closer friends, who knew me as an often-distracted woman who undertook too many things and left too little time to accomplish them, were less surprised to hear that I flew to India without any money. I forgot to get cash at the airport ATMs in Madison and Chicago, and when I inserted my credit card upon landing at New Delhi's Indira Gandhi International Airport, it was rejected. "Expired."

Susan, weary from the long flight, looked at me, brows furrowed.

"You don't have any money?" she asked me, voice flat.

"Didn't you bring any money?" I tossed the question back.

"A hundred dollars in traveler's checks," she said and glared.

"Oh, Susan," I sighed, exasperated, as if this were her fault. "No one uses traveler's checks anymore."

"You said you were going to pay for everything," she fired back, viewing with a frown the melee of Indian porters, international backpackers, and smartly dressed pilots and stewards streaming by. Was it only yesterday she had had both feet in Wisconsin, safe on the green grasses of a Madison summer?

I chuckled, my typical first reaction in a crisis, seeing the irony. Instead of rich, white Americans coming to walk among India's one billion masses, we would ourselves be two of the penniless. Not only did we have neither dollars nor rupees, we lacked a few of the basic tools needed to navigate another culture, unfamiliar with India's languages, practices, and religions. Our journey abroad had abruptly changed from picnic to panic, and for the remaining weeks of our travels, Susan's expressions harbored a vestige of betrayal. She added me to her list of disasters just waiting to implode.

I found an international telephone and made a collect call to my next-door neighbor Marilyn, telling her where she could probably find a new Visa card in my pile of unopened mail. "Send it express!" I urged, and gave her the address of Tenzin's sister, Dickey, in Delhi.

We needn't have worried. Tamdin, together with Dickey's good-humored husband, Damdul, met us amidst the bustle in the arrival lounge. From that moment on, even when my credit card arrived via international Federal Express a couple of days later, it was difficult to spend a single rupee. Meals had been planned, taxis ordered, bus tickets purchased, museum entries paid, modest hostels reserved.

"Oh, no," Namgyal and Tamdin would say, shaking their heads whenever I reached into my backpack to retrieve my wallet, "this is our country. You are our guest." They beamed magnanimously. Thus began a complex dance, as we would repeatedly weigh the acceptance of face-saving generosity with gentle negotiations for a more equitable balance of payments. I felt what it was like to be always on the receiving end. I tried to find humility, while people who had smaller bank accounts, but larger hearts and deeper traditions of hospitality, guided us along paths I never would have found without them.

~

In 2006, Delhi was a city of 12 million people. But as night fell, the taxi ride from the airport took us through a dark city with few lights. One cop directed twelve lanes of traffic as we turned out of the airport. Similar to big cities I had seen in my travels to Nepal, Thailand, and Morocco, Delhi appeared full of half-built buildings jammed together, or half-built buildings already collapsed into rubble.

The taxi was air-conditioned, so when I stepped out, my glasses fogged in the evening's humidity. It was eighty degrees, the coolest part of the day. Susan and I walked across a highway bridge, while Tamdin and Damdul shouldered my backpack and pulled Susan's roller suitcase. We stepped carefully over uneven cement, squinting against the darkness, and proceeded down a series of shadowy alleys, past men sitting beneath a bridge and in front of tiny shops, closed for the day.

Then Tamdin pushed open a door, and immediately we were met with bright lights and a squeal of delight as Dickey rushed toward us with outstretched arms.

"*Tashi delek. Tashi delek,*" she greeted us, using the Tibetan greeting that translates roughly as "blessings and good luck." "Welcome! You've arrived! We've all been waiting for you."

Dickey, short and plump with waist-length hair, lived smack in the middle of Delhi's sprawling Tibetan refugee community. By the end of our trip, after we had passed three times through Delhi, the words Dickey and Delhi would become synonyms for me. At this moment, Susan and I were simply relieved to relax into her warm embrace.

We hadn't expected to arrive in the midst of a death ritual, however. Dickey and Tenzin's father, the same grandfather who had gone with Thardoe to what had turned out to be his last Kalachakra, had passed away just weeks before. As I stepped into Dickey's yellow-plastered entryway, I heard a voice loudly chanting and the tinkling of small bells. For the first week after Tsewang Paldon's death, seven monks had been at Dickey's house around the clock, marking the start of the forty-nine-day Tibetan Buddhist mourning period. Now, just one monk came each day, filling the offering bowls before the special shrine, said to keep the house pure even during the time of death. He refilled the bowls with fresh water and molded *thorma*, which were intriguing, triangular shapes that he shaped from *tsampa* flour, Tibetan dry cheese (*churra*), butter, milk, and brown sugar.

The monk, a bald, older man with glasses, sat cross-legged on a bed in a bedroom that had been converted to an altar room. He beat a drum to begin prayers and alternately rang sets of bronze, brass, and silver bells. He proceeded through a hundred written prayers, at times droning with hands clasped, at other times humming along with what sounded like a second, sing-song voice.

"Is that recorded music?" I whispered to Dickey.

"No," she whispered back, "it's his 'two voices' he learned through his years of training."

How could we not have known of the death in the family, and in particular this very family we were joining for our visit? Doesn't family, by definition, include those first privy to news of impending births, deaths, and weddings? Perhaps I was not family in that respect yet, but I was mystified and alarmed by not being told about this important passing. Tibetan Buddhism is exalted for its knowledge, comfort, and philosophy to guide the dying. It seemed an unfortunate time to be ignorant.

Susan and I glanced at the monk as we walked past the altar room and followed Dickey to the living room. Despite the solemn religious rite taking place, household business proceeded.

As we seated ourselves on the living room sofa cushions, Dickey and Damdul reached for their cell phones and spoke in enthusiastic Tibetan, making one call after another.

"Yes, they are here. Yes, the plane arrived on time. Yes, we'll come visit you tomorrow. Yes, everything is good," I surmised they were saying.

When I tried to offer condolences, Dickey smiled. "Everyone dies," she said. "He had a healthy death. He lived a long time." I learned a healthy death means one has died with no fear and without people around exhibiting distracting grief. A healthy death meant he had died in a state of joy, vital for the situation into which he would next be born.

"Milk tea or butter tea?" asked a young Indian woman, Arusha, who turned out to be one of the family's two servants.

Susan and I nodded. "Either one, thanks," I said.

A few minutes later, a twelve-year-old Indian boy named Ranjit brought out four steaming cups, two for Susan and two for me. Arusha and Ranjit went in and out of the tiny kitchen just across from the bedroom where the monk was praying and reappeared with platters heaped with food. We ate white rice, mutton curry with freshly ground hot sauce (*siben mandu*), a Tibetan-style vegetable chow mein, and a fresh salad with a zingy dressing. After we had been enjoying dish after dish for a full hour, Arusha proudly set an enormous platter of *shammo*, mushrooms and chickpeas, before us, as if the cooks in the kitchen were getting down to serious business.

"Stop! Stop!" I laughed, protesting. "It's delicious, but we cannot eat any more."

The monk droned on. I got up and tiptoed to the doorway to see the ceremony from closer range, but he waved me away. They were serious and sacred, these ancient, complex steps to help the soul of Tsewang Paldon transit *bardo*, the intermediate state between life and rebirth. I had overstepped a boundary of respect: this was no tourist activity or spectator sport for curious, amateur anthropologists.

Dickey told me the day before our arrival, she, Damdul, and relatives had delivered one hundred *tsok*, or gifts—packets containing fruit, snacks, and a small ball of barley paste topped with a natural red dye, *moktsi*—to all throughout the dense neighborhood, asking for their blessing of Grandfather's spirit on its path to rebirth. On the forty-ninth day, they again made the deliveries, but this time with twice as many packets to three hundred neighbors. Kindness, generosity, and other meritorious actions during life, and by one's family during the days of mourning, help move one's spirit through the transition between life and death, to choose new parents, who will give the person his or her next body, in whatever living form.

Long past midnight, Tamdin and Damdul led Susan and me down darker alleys to Holiday Home, a former monastery, now a guesthouse largely patronized by traveling monks. We tiptoed up dark stairs to a room on the second floor and fumbled for a switch to the single hanging bulb. With relief, Susan turned on a rumbling air conditioner, and we stretched out on thin pallets, congruent with my idea of how parsimonious monks might sleep. The tiny room was more than adequate for our first night in India, a bit of privacy and away from the grandfather's lingering soul.

～

Susan and I had hoped to see Delhi's art and history museums, but these were not a part of our host families' daily lives. Instead, we were swept into their pace and destinations, not always sure where we were heading or why.

In every direction in the patchwork of connected apartments, neighbors knew Dickey, which meant they knew her sister Tenzin in America, which meant they had heard of me, Tenzin's "sponsor," as I was introduced. I found it disconcerting

that so many people I had never heard of before seemed somehow familiar with me, my Wisconsin lifestyle, and my role in
Tenzin's family. In an extended family, connected by frequent
international phone calls, I was apparently part of the narrative.
I stepped across invisible boundaries of acceptance, inclusion,
hospitality, and ignorance, stumbling occasionally.

During the next days, we paid courtesy calls to a round of
neighbors and relatives. The first visit was to Dickey and Tenzin's older half-sister, Acha (which means "older sister") Lhamo,
whose name was actually Tseten Lhamo, and her husband, Pema
Khando. Acha Lhamo's apartment was arranged exactly as
Dickey's nearby and Tenzin's in Madison—three oversized,
comfortable sofas buried in pillows set in a U shape, with a hos-
pitable coffee table in the middle for the requisite tea cups and
hot-water canisters. Why hadn't I troubled myself to learn, even
that morning, expressions of condolence?

The personal story of Khando, who was called Khando-lak
out of respect for his years, was similar to that of Migmar and so
many other men of the same age. Like Migmar, Khando-lak left
Tibet in 1959, though from a different village. He too escaped
over the snowy Himalayas and spent twenty years in the Indo-
Tibetan unit of India's Special Frontier Force, waiting for orders
to attack China, orders that never came. "In the early years,
hopes for regaining Tibet ran high," he told us, squinting over
thick, black, plastic-rimmed glasses. "Hopes remain, even now."

The struggle against the injustice of being run out of a homeland was the thread that ran through the life of every Tibetan
refugee I met. As a middle-class American, I had the luxury of
choosing my causes; Tibetans were born with one.

⁓

Acha Lhamo and Khando-lak took us outside and squatted to
point to a red line painted down the crumbling sidewalk. This

was the dividing line to indicate where the Tibetan settlement was to be torn down and replaced by a highway that Delhi badly needed, part of an undertaking called the Yamuna River Beautification Project. Acha Lhamo's apartment was on the side to be torn down; just across the line, Dickey's apartment would remain. The refugee settlement was known as New Arun Nagar Colony. It was in Delhi's Majnu-ka-tilla section, which was nestled between the Yamuna River and Delhi's Outer Ring Road and had a Sufi and Sikh history dating back to the 1400s. When the first refugees from Tibet took up residence as squatters in Majnu-ka-tilla, the area was being developed for resettlement by residents of northern Delhi. The refugees threw together rough shacks of bamboo and canvas. They later built brick homes and modest, canvas-roofed family businesses, which variously sold incense, medicinal herbs, traditional clothing, or antiques and treasures of Buddhism. With the addition of Internet cafés, travel agencies, tiny restaurants with inexpensive fare, and a small monastery and Buddhist temple, Majnu-ka-tilla grew popular with university students and tourists.

Our arrival coincided with heated discussions and despair over the city's plans to reclaim the land. Delhi's Tibetans, hurled first from their homeland, then from temporary refugee camps, were to be moved yet again, their culture and customs destined to be further diluted and dispersed. As our hosts explained to us what was happening, Susan and I exchanged uncomfortable glances: how could we drink butter tea as our hosts' livelihoods were imperiled?

As we visited neighbors and relatives, urgent conversations swirled around us in Tibetan. At first we thought they were about the impending eviction, and we shuffled uneasily. Then everyone turned to beam at us, and we found out they had been buzzing about a scheduled public ceremony to be officiated by the Dalai Lama in Dharamsala, northern India. Not only that, but we ourselves were going to travel to witness it. (Some years later, I was relieved to hear that the other topic of conversation du jour—the neighborhood to be torn down—had not transpired after all.)

Tamdin had just returned from the bus station where he had purchased first-class bus tickets for himself, Susan, and me. He mentioned Namgyal was already there, as well as Thardoe, of course, and that we would depart tomorrow. The Hindi script on the bus tickets that Tamdin proudly handed to us said "500 rupees." Five hundred seemed excessive, but it was only ten dollars at that year's exchange rate.

Since these were first-class tickets for a journey of twelve to fourteen hours, Susan and I expected something like a Greyhound bus. The air conditioner turned out to be a couple of noisy fans, only the fans didn't work. At least the windows opened, but that let in fumes of fertilizer plants, cow dung, and diesel exhaust. We had packed books to read after dark, since the bus would travel through the night, but the night lights didn't work. As the dusk deepened, we nonetheless found plenty to look at from our windows. Every imaginable mode of transport shared our road—bicycles piled with hay, auto rickshaws carrying two women and ten children in seats meant for three, horse-drawn carts piled with bricks and lumber, and city buses with bald, underinflated tires, packed to bursting with what looked like a hundred men.

I watched Susan look out her window. I had traveled through less economically developed countries before, but what could she be thinking about all of this? Were her fears of impending dangers being confirmed or dispelled?

The bus passed a sick, bony woman with a thin child in her arms, sleeping on a sidewalk. Ten half-built apartment buildings stood side by side in a halted construction project, with piles of bricks, dirt, and boulders left in the middle of the highway for traffic to veer around. Alongside every road we saw a panorama of men washing, spitting, sipping tea, fixing flats, playing *korram*, or sleeping in every possible position in their vehicles while they waited for the next fare or next load.

The bus moved forward at a bumpy crawl. The bus driver seemed to honk the horn through the late afternoon, through the night, and into the next morning, to barrel past bicycles, sheep, Brahmin bulls, and all smaller vehicles. The driver made two stops where there were toilets and a restaurant, but then drove eight hours, barely slowing down in town centers, as new passengers boarded. Men jumped off and back on the bus to pee against stone walls, while we women looked at one another in dismay. We frowned and crossed our legs tighter as the bus lurched onward. (I remembered from an earlier trek seeing women in Nepal, in long, full skirts, simply step back a bit from a crowd, and when they moved forward again, there would be a wet spot in the sand. Dressing like local women had practical as well as social advantages.) We slept in fits.

At daybreak, the bus started climbing into the foothills of the Himalayas. The foliage had grown thick outside, and through the trees we glimpsed monkeys and waterfalls. Just as we got within Dharamsala city limits, the road narrowed and a traffic jam converged. On either side of the road, cars inched past cement drainage ditches that were two feet deep. I stared nervously at a precipice that plunged dangerously, seeming to be just inches from the bus's wheels. On the other side of the bus, cars squeezed past, separated from us by what looked like millimeters. I shut my eyes—there would be safer vistas from which to view the snowy peaks that had suddenly emerged ahead. The passengers burst into relieved applause as the bus, honking victoriously, burst into the main center of Dharamsala.

Tamdin hurried Susan and me off the bus and flagged down a taxi. We climbed in, and now it was this taxi that honked its way past cows and schoolchildren in the middle of the road, until we finally reached a regal, ancient monastery. Was this where we would be staying? It looked like a Buddhist equivalent of the Vatican.

I tried to ask Tamdin, but he brushed aside my questions. "Later, later," he said.

We knew we were in an immense hurry when no tea was offered. A second taxi came and took us to the top of a farther hill, where His Holiness the Dalai Lama was beginning a three-hour initiation ceremony. It seemed everyone in town, all eight thousand of them, plus a hundred-strong delegation from Taiwan, plus hundreds of Buddhism students and wide-eyed tourists from all around the world—surely more than ten thousand people in all—had gathered here. We had arrived precisely on time, not quite sure what to expect from this seemingly momentous event. Nonetheless, Susan and I sighed with relief. We had been away from our Wisconsin cottage for less than a week, but it seemed we were on a Tibetan-Indian roller coaster, out of control of all that was ordinary and familiar.

Susan and I melded into the audience of red-robed nuns and monks, Tibetan women wearing long *chupa* skirts and brightly striped aprons, some younger pink- and blue-haired tourists with tattoos and backpacks, and the two of us in our longish skirts and sandals. With so many fascinating things to take in, I barely noticed that the entire proceedings were in Tibetan. Initiates in the ceremony had participated for two and a half weeks to learn particular teachings from the *Guide to the Bodhisattva Way of Life,* a text written by the eighth-century Indian Buddhist monk Shantideva. Gongs gonged, bells rang, monks chanted. The audience joined in on certain prayers; I thought it was thunder when it began as a low rumble, but when I glanced back, I noted it was the older people, not the younger ones or foreigners, who intoned fervently. I craned my head to spot Namgyal and Thardoe. I was sure they were somewhere in the crowd but didn't see them.

To attend an authentic Tibetan Buddhist ceremony in Madison requires leaving the busy city center and driving out into the country to Deer Park Temple. Here, Buddhist practice and ceremony seemed to be in the air, on the ground, in the winds. We inhaled it.

Susan and I sat on the ground under the hot sun, just two among many, and watched the proceedings simultaneously on the stage and on a large television screen to the side. At the end of each section of the three-hour ceremony, monks carrying large silver buckets passed through the crowd, the first time giving us small balls of sweet, cooked barley, called *tseril*; the next time sugary, hot rice with raisins, called *dre sil*, which we ate from cupped hands; then finally, fried donuts cut into small pieces. Like loaves and fishes, the food was dispensed into a sea of outstretched hands and seemed to be enough to feed everyone.

At the end of the ceremony, the Dalai Lama passed through the crowd just inches from us and gave Tamdin, Susan, and me a big smile, as if he had been expecting us and was pleased we had arrived. I was shaken. The great man passed into another building, and Tamdin said the ceremony was over. Nothing stopped being fascinating, however. Tamdin led us down stony paths back to the monastery. Susan and I stepped carefully lest we slip, while old women, monks of all ages, and boisterous children wearing flip-flops ran down the same steps. I looked back. With handmade brooms, robed nuns, their heads shaved bald, were bent double to clean the ground, sweeping away the few grains of rice and crumbs left by the worshippers.

~

I had started the day on a bumpy bus, then was greeted by His Holiness the Dalai Lama in a crowd of thousands, and now was wondering how on earth Susan and I had come to stay on the grounds of a sacred monastery. We appeared to be the only non-Buddhist, non-Tibetan, non-monk, non-male guests. We humbly tiptoed up a flight of stairs to the small room that had been assigned to us.

Tamdin had said a few words to the man in the downstairs kiosk that sold orange drink and chewing gum. Then he abruptly left, mentioning that he and Namgyal were staying at the Tibetan Library Guest House nearby, but failing to explain where we were or why he had chosen this holy place for our lodging. The four-story, brick monastery guesthouse was bathed in rays of sunlight. A pamphlet beside our narrow beds informed us that Nechung Monastery was rebuilt in 1977, following the destruction during China's Cultural Revolution of the monastery in Tibet after which this one was named. Monastery history went back to the eighth century CE, when succeeding oracles in the Tibetan temple were appointed not only to be protector of the country's Buddhist religion, but also protector of the entire Tibetan government, furthermore, responsible for peace and harmony on earth.

Was it shallow, even disrespectful, to explore Tibetan culture without delving into its spiritual side? After all, why did Tibetans want to "free Tibet" if not for the freedom to practice their centuries-old religion? The language, festivals, foods, and austere landscape could not be separated from the religion. Was I using Unitarians' blanket acceptance of world religions as an excuse not to probe more deeply into multitudinous strata of Buddhist beliefs?

Growing up, I had attended Unitarian Sunday school, but even as a child I had been suspicious of the convenience of a fellowship that didn't meet in the summer because "too many people were on vacation." The small group of Unitarians in our medium-sized Oklahoma city attracted a handful of Jews, Buddhists, and Hindus, as well as a potpourri of spiritual free thinkers. In Sunday school I learned about the world's great religions, no one more ascendant than any other. My stepmother once taught science experiments in the Sunday school class of younger students. My spirituality included reverence for the magnificence of nature and for all that science explores, that poetry celebrates, and that literature and philosophy reflect upon.

Many aspects of Buddhism beckoned me. I loved the Dalai Lama's quiet wisdom and courageous pacifism. From a distance, I admired friends who meditated and practiced yoga. I liked Buddhism's built-in role for skeptics, its centuries-old rich oral traditions, its focus on simplicity and nonmaterialism, and its lack of worship of a single deity. I liked the magnificent icons and artistry of its altars. No one among my Tibetan American family or their relatives ever tried to convert me or encourage me to attend teachings. Like the religions of Native American peoples, I knew the learner must first show herself worthy. I was tiptoeing about the edges, not yet ready.

As I lay on the simple mattress, I wondered if perhaps the monk who held the title Venerable Kuten (Oracle) Thupten Ngodup was also falling asleep in his room in the attached monastery. The job description of his predecessors had included "responsibility for peace and harmony on earth." What if I had been raised among people who believed the future could be predicted, that suffering could cease, that peace on earth was achievable? Sleep descended, and I dreamed I was wandering as a robed nun, a woman of simple possessions, a healer.

～

In the days that followed, I was drawn into Dharamsala's ubiquitous harmonies. People around us chanted, incense wafted from shops and temples, and prayer flags fluttered from every tree, sending wishes for peace and compassion to the heavens. Susan and I began attending Buddhist lectures, something we had never pursued at home.

We joined thirty other foreigners from various European, Australian, and North American countries in a monastery classroom. The others had signed up for a two-and-a-half-day study of a single sutra, or scripture verse, *Sutra of Exalted Wisdom of Going Beyond.* A red-robed monk, Geshé Sonam Rinchen, sat at an altar. Geshé, we had learned, is an honorific title that designates a person as "professor" or "master." A white woman from New Zealand, maybe in her forties, dressed in a modest denim skirt, exquisitely translated his quiet words, her accent soothing in the dimly lit room.

"Be compassionate," Geshé Sonam Rinchen explained the sutra. "What kind of mind cultivates compassion? A mind that is clear light. Sunlight falls on a diamond, sunlight falls on dung. That it falls on dung does not rob the sunlight of its nature, its clarity. Even if we are reborn an insect, it does not affect the clarity of our mind."

How many people, over how many centuries, had reflected upon these words? Blessings surrounded us, free for the taking. Wisdom could not be had without listening, without reading, without reflecting—but it, too, was there for the taking.

The lesson continued. "Water is pure. It can be distilled of pollutants. Gold is pure. Alloys can be refined from it. Similarly, our mind is pure. Misery and impure thoughts are temporary. They can be removed. Look for Buddha within yourself."

The Buddha within me was my goodness, my caring spirit, my creativity. It was the unselfish part that enabled me to reach out to children, women, and men who passed through my days. They awaited my touch, and I could receive theirs, but not without being vulnerable or willing to experience loss. The

Buddha within me had beckoned me here to sense the powers of love and loss, and the beauty of emptiness and letting go. My spiritual pores, shut tight to mysticism, opened a little to the gentle wisdom.

Maybe it wasn't just Thardoe whom Tenzin had sent to India to learn about his Tibetan heritage. Maybe she had sent me, too, to find my gentler self.

(*above*) Tenzin Kalsang in Old Camp 1, Bylakuppe, India, with children Namgyal, Tamdin, and Thardoe. MIGMAR DORJEE FAMILY COLLECTION

(*left*) Tenzin Kalsang and Migmar Dorjee with their four children, Namgyal, Lhadon, Tamdin, and Thardoe, in Bylakuppe, India, in 1992. MIGMAR DORJEE FAMILY COLLECTION

Brothers Tamdin and Thardoe in the Bylakuppe settlement's cooperatively owned cornfield in 1994. MIGMAR DORJEE FAMILY COLLECTION

In May 1998, the family took their first outing with Madeline Uraneck, to Milwaukee's Veteran's Memorial Park. From right: Lhadon, Thardoe, Migmar, Tenzin, Namgyal, and Tamdin (sitting).

Tenzin Kalsang and Migmar Dorjee pause for a tea break in their laundry room "office" at Kennedy Manor, in Madison, Wisconsin.

(*left*) Tenzin Kalsang polishes an elevator in Kennedy Manor, where she started working in 1995.

(*below*) Tenzin Kalsang , second from right, and an unidentified Somali woman at their citizenship ceremony in 1999.

Brothers Tamdin and Thardoe with Madeline at Indian Lake County Park, in Dane County, Wisconsin, in 1999.

Tenzin Kalsang poses before her family's Losar shrine, which on this year included a pile of homemade *khapse* (sweets), fruit, and a bottle of whiskey, all adorned with *khata* (scarves) to bless the new year. Tibetan Americans across the nation celebrate Losar, the Tibetan new year, which often falls in February.

Genlak Jampa Khedup, one of the five teachers at the Wisconsin Tibetan Association's Saturday School, drills older kids, all born in the United States and fluent in English, in phonetics of the Tibetan alphabet. Many Tibetan Americans in Madison send their children to the school to learn the language, culture, and history of their ancestral country.

Lhadon and Thardoe celebrate their sixteenth and fourteenth birthdays jointly with an American-style party in June 2000, at Madeline's cabin. The children had not celebrated birthdays in the refugee settlment in India. MIGMAR DORJEE FAMILY COLLECTION

Ani Pachen (1933–2002), a Tibetan-Buddhist nun who suffered imprisonment and torture during a twenty-one-year sentence in Chinese prisons, passed through Madison, Wisconsin, in February 2000, to promote her autobiography, *Sorrow Mountain: The Remarkable Story of a Tibetan Warrior Nun*.

(*above*) Thardoe, Lhadon, and Tamdin run down the dunes in Nehalem Bay State Park to view the ocean for the first time. The three accompanied Madeline on a 2001 Thanksgiving visit to her brother and sister in Oregon.

(*left*) Lhadon, second from right, pictured with friends at East High School in Madison during Fine Arts Week, 2001.

(*above*) Tenzin Kalsang with her only daughter, Lhadon.

(*left*) Tenzin Kalsang with son Thardoe at his citizenship ceremony in Milwaukee, 2002.

Tenzin (right) and neighbor Phurbu Sangmo make *momo* (Tibetan-style dumplings) for a Thanksgiving celebration with Madeline. Sitting on the floor, the family could quickly roll one hundred momo in a variety of shapes for holidays and special events.

Tamdin's 2003 high school graduating class included a large number of Tibetan American peers. Proud parents, including Migmar Dorjee, honored this first generation of their US-raised children by placing *khata* around their necks as a blessing.

(*left*) Joining students of Tibetan ethnicity from many countries, Thardoe studied an ancient religious art at the Institute of Tibetan Thangka Arts in Dharamsala, India, from August 2005 to July 2006. He was permitted to try to paint a *thangka*, although typical study of this tradional style of painting takes five years.

(*below*) When Tenzin Kalsang's father passed away in 2006, monks performed forty-nine days of prayers and ceremonies in the home of Tenzin's sister, Dickey Norzom, in Delhi, India. According to Tibetan Buddhism, these rituals help the soul of the deceased on its way to its next life.

In 2006, eight years after they had left for the United States, the three brothers, Namgyal, Thardoe, and Tamdin, returned to visit their former house in Old Camp 1 near Bylakuppe, India. Families who fled Tibet were alloted a modest house, built by early arrivals to the refugee settlement.

Madeline with her sister Susan in Dharamsala. The two were accompanied by brothers Namgyal, Tamdin, and Thardoe as guides and translators on their shared travels from north to south India in summer 2006.

(*above*) Namgyal met Lhakpa Dolma, his future wife, on the 2006 trip to Dharamsala. "If they wish to marry, neither of our families will object," said Lhakpa's brother-in-law, who had assisted with the informal, cross-continental matchmaking. This day hike to Dharamkot was chaperoned by Madeline, her sister, and the brother-in-law.

(*left*) After an initiation ceremony in Dharamsala, northern India, officiated by the Dalai Lama, monks pass through the crowd to offer everyone *dre sil*, or sweet rice.

Namgyal cuts and decorates cookies in Madeline's Wisconsin kitchen for Christmas in 2013.

Whatever the weather, Migmar Dorjee often steps out onto his porch to roast barley, a key ingredient for *tsampa*, a Tibetan staple food.

Groom Tenzin Dechen and bride Nawang Lhadon, at their 2013 wedding celebration in Jampaling Tibetan Settlement, near Pokhara, Nepal. Lhadon's traditional *shamo gasse* (hat) is lined with fox fur.

After her wedding, Lhadon traveled with her husband, relatives, and Madeline to several famous Buddhist temples in Nepal, where they prayed, did circular *kora* (temple walks), lit candles, and strung prayer flags from trees at sacred sites.

Migmar Dorjee and Tenzin Kalsang, wearing their traditional Tibetan-style *chupa*.
PETER WILLIAMS

CHAPTER 8

◦

Revelations in India

Certainly travel is more than the seeing of sights; it is a change that goes on, deep and permanent, in the ideas of living.
— MIRIAM RITTER BEARD, AMERICAN HISTORIAN

Still suffering from jet lag, Susan and I sometimes fell asleep without dinner. One evening in the monastery guesthouse, we were awakened about 7 p.m. to the sound of the monks chanting their evening prayers. The chanting continued for an hour, then for two hours after that, the monks assembled in the courtyard beneath our windows to hold *tse-nyi Rigba* dialectics, or verbal debates. I got out of bed and watched forty pairs of shaved, red-robed young monks, one of the pair sitting on the cement steps, the other standing in front of him. The standing one, with a role similar to "devil's advocate," clapped, stomped, and swung his prayer beads over his arm as he questioned, challenged, and refuted the points put forth by the sitting defender.

The next day, Thardoe's host father, Wangdu, explained to us that this was the monks' way of studying the teachings of Buddhist sutras and tantric texts and exploring ancient questions: What is truth? What is enlightenment? The process was governed by specific progressions, defined rules, and precise time constraints, all done under the watchful eyes of head lamas. Each clapping gesture had a meaning, some identifiable with different monasteries. For instance, the debater struck his out-reached left palm with his right palm to begin a new line of questioning. When a question was answered correctly, the debater brought the back of his right hand to his left palm. Clapping hands loudly connoted the power and exactness of the argument, as well as the confidence of the defender.

Each monk was concentrating hard, focused intently on the words of the monk facing him. Lamas wandered among the pairs, stopping to listen or interrupt. Sometimes this kind of debate was done as practice, other times as competition. Through a process of elimination at certain festivals or ceremonies, debating monks advanced to argue with other accomplished students. As a curriculum designer, I tried to picture a US social studies class using this method to debate global issues. The ancient, learner-to-learner instruction offered an interesting model to contemporary educators.

The three brothers—indeed, most Tibetans back in Madison—were familiar with the story of the brilliant young scholar, Lhundub Sopa, who entered Sera Monastery in Lhasa, Tibet, and participated in many hours of these *tse-nyi Rigba* dialectics as part of his studies. Even before Lhundub Sopa completed his own examinations, he was chosen as one of the Dalai Lama's debate examiners during the annual Prayer Festival in 1949 in Lhasa. Years later, when he was known as Geshé Sopa, he was encouraged by the Dalai Lama to go to the United States to learn English and teach Americans and Tibetan refugees who wished to further their religious studies.

In 1967, Geshé Sopa was invited to join the pioneering Buddhist studies program at the University of Wisconsin–Madison. There he attracted admiring, devoted students and mentored a new generation of Buddhist studies scholars. With

Geshé Sopa's vision and leadership, Madison's Deer Park Buddhist Center was constructed in 1975, its elegant architecture stunning in the verdant setting south of Madison, and he became its founding abbot. Whenever the Dalai Lama visited Madison, Deer Park was his residence. A small group of monks and nuns lived full time at the center and led weekly services and teachings; Buddhists and religious scholars from all over the region, the nation, and many other countries toured its grounds and temple. The Kalachakra held there was not only the first in North America, but first in the entire western hemisphere.

I had caught glimpses of the Venerable Geshé Sopa, or Geshelak, as many called him, at Tibetan-Buddhist events in Madison. With his big smile he was easy to recognize, always surrounded by a retinue of monks. At the time of his death in 2014 at age ninety-one, he was revered by Buddhists, scholars, and ordinary people across several continents, having strengthened fragile strings of peace, scholarship, religion, and community.

Here in Dharamsala, in the monastery courtyard, I had a glimpse of what his training would have looked like. How far would the young scholars beneath my window travel? What future leaders would their rigorous training inspire? Even though Geshé Sopa was one of Madison's esteemed citizens, it wasn't until I journeyed to India that I began to comprehend his path and contributions. There was something magical in contemplating the distances that philosophical teachings could travel. The monastery's prayer flags, linked by a tenuous string, blew in the evening breezes, sending prayers to the heavens. Similarly, I was tied to my Tibetan family by what felt like diaphanous threads, just as they and I were connected to the wisdom of sages who had long preceded us, connections delicate, yet enduring.

～

Down a side street in Dharamsala, Susan and I found the Tibet Museum, which in those days was small and underfunded. Unlike now, its permanent exhibits were few in number, mostly photos, newspaper articles, and displays of religious artifacts, but even so the collective impression was powerful: China's occupation of Tibet, the dramatic journey into exile for so many thousands of people, the daily life of exiled Tibetans in many different countries captured in photographs, and tributes to His Holiness the Dalai Lama from world leaders and luminous dignitaries. Groups of children and young monks gathered around various panels. For them, this history was living and personal.

All year, Thardoe had been hosted by a remarkable young couple, Wangdu and his wife, Tsamchoe. From the museum where she worked, Tsamchoe guided Susan and me upstairs to in the Library of Tibetan Works and Archives. As we stepped into the low-lit room of the library, our eyes rose to the ceilings. Tall, custom-built shelves held scriptures wrapped in yellow cloth and brocade. Drawers archived tens of thousands of rare photographs and images, which rotated through special exhibits in the museum. Archives staff photographed and digitized ancient scriptures to make them available on CD-ROM to a worldwide community of monks, scholars, and ordinary Tibetans.

She introduced us to the curator of the rare manuscript section, who told us about the effort to reassemble lost artifacts. From the Chinese invasion in the late 1950s through China's Cultural Revolution in the 1960s, millions of pages of Tibetan scriptures and sutras, poems, written music, woodblock prints, frescoes, *thangkas*, and entire encyclopedias of medicine, ethics, aesthetics, science, and ancient practices had been destroyed. During 1966 and 1967 alone, the mass student paramilitary social movement called the Red Guards bashed remaining statues of Buddha and hauled away religious texts to be shredded for mud wall cement, used as toilet paper, or scattered to the winds. Now people like the curator—librarians, historians, and esteemed Tibetologists—collect and piece together rare texts that had been smuggled out by those fleeing, often tucked into sleeves or wrapped in burlap in the modest bags they carried, or buried along the escape route.

"From time to time," the curator said, "a new scripture shows up. Perhaps it was smuggled out of a monastery, or even stolen, and now someone wants to return it or sell it to the library." To save a culture, diaspora Tibetans were not only collecting such objects but also starting Saturday schools and summer camps for children, conducting workshops in monastery settings, and sending selected masters, like the once-chosen Geshé Sopa, to instruct Tibetans living throughout the diaspora as well as other professors and practitioners. While I felt awe and relief at the immensity and organization of the effort, I also sensed the impossibility of transporting an always-morphing culture, with so many intangible aspects, from one place to another. The transitions in language and prayers and even foods in my own Madison family were caught up in these winds.

Tsamchoe saw me staring at a color photo in which a group of seven people straggled across a snowy pass.

"People are walking that route as we speak," Tsamchoe said quietly.

That single sentence suddenly linked past to present for me. It wasn't just Migmar and other elders who had crossed the peaks as teens. Teens were still crossing the peaks. Millions of refugees in other countries, too, were making harrowing journeys, swept along in vicious, political avalanches. I looked out the museum window at the mountains in the distance, squinting as if to discern tiny specks in the snow.

Because the Chinese government does not allow ethnic Tibetans to leave or enter the Tibetan Autonomous Region without permission, the flow across borders continues to be illegal.

"If we are traveling to Tibet from here," Tsamchoe explained, "and we are caught once by the Chinese border police, we might be warned or jailed briefly. If we're caught twice, we're jailed a long time. Still, we Tibetans who live outside Tibet perhaps want to see our parents one last time. Or maybe we want to search for our siblings who remained behind when we fled. And people with businesses need to bring back handicrafts for sale."

The traffic flows both ways. When ethnic Tibetans wish to flee China, they find a guide, usually Nepali, who takes a considerable sum of money to lead them on a route across mountains that might border Bhutan, India, or Nepal.

Everyone we met had an escape story, and Tsamchoe's husband, Wangdu, told Susan and me this one: In 1998, a mother and a father in Tibet brought their eight-year-old son, small for his age, to a guide. They paid the guide and begged him to take good care of their son, and then they cried as they parted, as if they suspected they might never see their child again.

The guide was leading a larger-than-usual group of about thirty people, which was perilous as it increased their risk of being caught. The escape took about two weeks. The two-day trek across a Himalayan pass made everyone particularly nervous, as they were out in the open—dark figures against white snow. They could easily be spotted by the border patrol and picked off with high-powered rifles. It was the most dangerous part of the journey, and the guide urged everyone to move faster.

From the beginning, the small boy had been a problem. The guide took no interest in him. Every day the boy lagged farther behind, and sometimes he simply sat down and cried.

"Leave him!" the guide barked at the adults nearest the boy on a day when haste would make a life-and-death difference.

One man, who didn't know the boy and wasn't related to him, felt unable to leave him to die in the cold. With the hardest days of climbing still ahead, and the anxiety of survival at its peak, the man picked up the boy, put him on his shoulders, and struggled through the huge drifts of snow.

The boy's savior would become one of Tsamchoe and Wangdu's friends. He worked in town as an artist at Norbulinka Institute of Tibetan Arts. The boy had grown to be a tall young man and was about to graduate from high school in Dharamsala. The man and the boy were close friends.

In an understated way that was becoming familiar to me in Tibetan circles, Wangdu ended the story with, "Our friend is a good man."

He was more than just "a good man." The instant in which he had swept the boy into his arms crystalized deep human ethics, the world's very goodness. The powerful fact that the two were not even related, and were friends still today, touched me. Who is our family? At what moment do we choose those to whom we will remain committed for the rest of our days?

Everywhere we turned in Dharamsala, Susan and I encountered groups of chattering children in school uniforms. We visited Lower Tibetan Children's Village (TCV) School, where one of Migmar's cousins was a teacher and her partner was employed as a live-in house parent. Had Namgyal, Lhadon, Tamdin, and Thardoe remained in India, at least some of them would have ended up in this school or one like it. On that day, eight hundred children were enrolled in the primary school, grades one to six. Up the hill, in Upper Tibetan Children's Village School, two thousand students in grades one to nine attended a combined primary and middle school. Secondary schools were attached to each one.

I asked Wangdu's cousin to explain the difference between Dharamsala's Upper and Lower TCV Schools. Children in the Lower School come from families that can pay the school fees,

she told me, while children in the Upper School are largely
scholarship students who were orphaned in, escaped from, or
smuggled out of Tibet. "Some of them," she said, "will never see
their parents again."

A Tibetan proverb says, "A child without an education is
like a bird without wings." I wondered how many parents in
the world would choose between their children's education
and never being able to see them again. To these parents, caught
in oppressive times, education was more than a road to their
children's future and a guarantee for their well-being: it was
an act of love, hope, and sacrifice in the struggle to keep Tibetan
dreams alive.

If they had parents or relatives nearby, children in the Lower
School went home on second and fourth weekends. In the Upper
School, however, most children had nowhere to go on week-
ends or holidays, and older children stepped forward to serve
as house parents for the smaller ones. Across the world, many
with and without Tibetan ties sent annual contributions to the
Upper Tibetan Children's Village School, and schools in other
TCV branches, to support the tuition and care of one child.

The curriculum in both schools emphasized instruction in
the Tibetan language in all subjects, with English and Hindi not
introduced until grades five and six. Teachers and parents felt it
imperative for children first to build a good foundation in their
heritage language. The Tibetan language was like a river that
melted from the Himalayan snows: its words and cadence carried a vast, imperiled culture—values, mores, medicine, songs,
folk tales, history, and prayers.

～

"Let's hike to Dharamkot," said Thardoe's host father, Wangdu.
"It's an old British hill station. Very pretty." We were in good
spirits as Susan and I set off with him. Thardoe stayed home to

work on his *thangka* painting, but Namgyal, Tamdin, and two sisters from a neighboring family, Lhakpa and Namdol, joined us. We carried a picnic in our daypacks. The cypress forest was thick and mossy, and prayer flags blew gently from primeval trees.

Namgyal and Lhakpa walked hand in hand at the front of our little group. Then I got it. I realized why Tenzin, back in the United States, had sent all her sons, together with me and my sister, on a sightseeing trip to India. We were not here to look at ancient temples and meet relatives; we were looking for wives! We were two mature American women serving as chaperones and lending credibility to the family's social standing back home.

I began to see clues I had missed. For instance, what better way to preserve the culture than to send the youngest son to spend an entire year in a place where he could meet dozens of young women of Tibetan ethnicity, from among whom he might choose a wife? If I had been a real Tibetan aunt, I would have been actively making calls and inquiries, as I was soon to realize Tenzin had been doing, to support her important and discerning matchmaking strategies.

I thought back: Namgyal had been beaming for days. Aha! This is why he had rushed ahead to Dharamsala and hadn't waited a few days for Susan and me to land at Delhi's airport. I looked more closely at Lhakpa, the young woman at his side. Maybe she wasn't just a neighbor girl along for our hike. Maybe she was a person who would become a part of my own life.

I panted as the path became steeper, while Wangdu walked easily beside me. "How did those two meet?" I asked him, my voice suspicious.

He smiled and recounted how, through Migmar and Tenzin's conversations with friends, cousins, and in-laws, Namgyal and Lhakpa had been chosen for one another. Wangdu had played a big part.

"I'm married to Tsamchoe, and Tsamchoe is Lhakpa's older sister," he said. "My brother is married to Dickey, Tenzin's sister. So when we'd meet Dickey's family in Delhi from time to time, we learned about these guys in America." It was natural that sooner or later, his wife's younger sisters would be mentioned as perfect in age, personality, and family background for Dickey's nephews in the United States.

Tenzin herself had actually met Lhakpa by chance a couple of years prior, while visiting Dickey in Delhi. Lhakpa and her sister Namdol were also in Delhi, accompanying their mother to receive treatments from a popular acupuncturist. As they sat side by side, waiting in line for their turn, Tenzin noticed the two daughters, both well dressed, polite, respectful, and reserved, their ages likely near those of her sons. From later inquiries to Dickey and her husband, Damdul, she learned Lhakpa and Namdol came from a well-respected family in Dharamsala; both women spoke excellent English and had college degrees.

Several years later, she showed Namgyal a photograph she had obtained in a roundabout fashion. "What do you think, Namgyal?" she asked. He studied the photo. Both sisters were slender, both had long black hair, both were dressed in their traditional New Year *Losar chupa*.

"This one looks too tall," he said, pointing to Namdol. "How old is she?"

Mother and son calculated that the tall one was two years older than he.

"This one." Namgyal pointed to Lhakpa.

⤳

The first time Wangdu told Lhakpa about Namgyal, a young Tibetan American in Wisconsin, she wasn't particularly interested. "I didn't tell any of my friends about him," Lhakpa confided in me later. "I thought I'd just wait and see."

But then Namgyal began calling her, almost every night, after he got home from his late-night job at the grocery store.

"I remember his first call," Lhakpa told me. "We had absolutely nothing to talk about. He asked me what were my favorite fruits. He said he liked mangos, and I said I liked oranges." She bent forward on the sofa, laughing hard with the memory. "Fruits!" she repeated. "Then he asked me if I had a hobby. I said cooking, and he said soccer. There was a long silence after that. It felt like we had nothing in common."

Namgyal's fervor mounted, however, even if I had completely missed it. And while Tamdin had escorted Susan and me around Delhi, Namgyal had raced ahead to Dharamsala to meet the woman of his fantasies and phone calls.

"If Namgyal and Lhakpa like one another, the two families have no objection to their marriage," Wangdu explained to me, as we continued on the mountain path.

So, this "arranged marriage" was not so much "arranged" as presented as a propitious, well-considered introduction. Parents on both sides were hopeful, but if one or both young people expressed disinclination, the introduction would come to naught. This was more than a mere introduction, however. Expensive plane and bus tickets transported the would-be groom to the young woman. And unlike the loose attempts at matchmaking associated with the American practice of blind dates, these two seemed to have commitment to the process and faith in the judgment of those who knew them best.

Namgyal had never dated in Madison, and I had once teased him about his high school girlfriends. He had replied seriously, "I don't need to date. I'll marry who my parents tell me." At the time I found this a startling assertion, but now here I was, watching Namgyal and Lhakpa walk hand in hand, myself a minor player in their romance. I wondered if Namgyal was feeling pressure but then answered my own question. I had never seen him appear so effusive, outgoing, or debonair.

On the trail behind the young couple and their siblings, Susan and I breathed harder as the incline increased. Wangdu told me that Tenzin, back in Madison, in phone conversations with his family, thought Namdol might be a good fit for Tamdin. We watched Tamdin and Namdol chase one another up and down the path and flirtatiously flick small pebbles at each other when we had stopped to rest. While the romance had sparks during our time in India, I heard later that the introduction did not catch fire, so the enchanting possibility of two brothers marrying two sisters smoldered and died.

Back in Madison, I had once asked Migmar, "What are the qualities of an ideal wife?"

He quickly listed off several things, as if he had given the topic much previous thought.

I asked Namgyal to translate.

"She should be very rich, fancy and modern and stuck-up, and she should have a very loud voice," Namgyal joked.

"No, what did he really say?" I persisted.

Namgyal and his brothers kept laughing at his witty translation, so Tenzin helped me. "She should be humble, respectful, educated, able to get along well with both sets of parents, and harmonious in groups." Later Migmar clarified that education wasn't as important as the other qualities. By any standard, Lhakpa seemed like a remarkable candidate.

I was once again impressed with Tenzin's ability to construct master plans for her children and her ability to create this win-win expedition, with Susan and me being thanked by multitudes of her relatives and at the same time cementing our footprints in her family's future paths.

I hadn't considered how this trip would introduce—and obligate—me to more people in Tenzin's extended family. I had not anticipated how my commitment to one team in the tug-of-war between Tibet and China would deepen. I hadn't figured how this journey would open spiritual doors that would challenge my worldview. I wondered what else Tenzin, and the karma she believed in, intended for me to see and understand.

CHAPTER 9

~

Back to Bylakuppe

Sometimes, reaching out and taking someone's hand is the beginning of a journey. At other times, it is allowing another to take yours.
—VERA NAZARIAN, RUSSIAN ARMENIAN AUTHOR

Throughout our visit, Thardoe continued attending his classes at Dharamsala's Institute of Tibetan Thangka Arts. But he had decided one year was enough; as a US citizen with a home in America, he had options. Most of his fellow students, by contrast, would labor four more years to complete the five-year training.

Students had arrived at the school from Tibetan diaspora communities throughout India, Mongolia, Bhutan, Nepal, Russia, and even the Tibetan Autonomous Region itself. They paid no tuition, and the two *thangka* masters, whom the students addressed as *genlak*, meaning "teacher," taught for free, doing their own artwork in the mornings and stopping by the institute several afternoons each week to offer instruction and critiques.

Susan and I hiked with Thardoe up Dharamsala streets early one morning to the home studio of one of the instructors, Genlak Tsering. Thardoe had in his pocket a folded *khata* to present to his teacher as thanks, and I had given him an envelope containing two hundred dollars. Genlak Tsering welcomed us into his modest home, the front room crowded with magnificent *thangka* paintings, stretched on canvas, some standing almost ceiling high. Thardoe draped the silken white *khata* over the man's neck, a blessing of appreciation and respect. Thardoe translated as Genlak Tsering told us how he had been born in Tibet in 1968 and had worked there as recently as 1987. The Chinese government, increasingly aware that Tibetan Buddhist temples were strong magnets for foreign tourists, had paid Genlak Tsering for restoration work. Since leaving Tibet for India, he had twice hiked back over the Himalayas to visit his family who remained there.

"The last time," he recounted, "I was caught by border guards and had all my ID cards confiscated. Now I'm listed as an enemy of the state. I can never return again. It's too risky." He looked away.

In his exiled life in India, Genlak Tsering and Thardoe's second teacher, Genlak Ngodup, kept busy with commissions. Their customers included monasteries, museums, art collectors, and Buddhists and diaspora Tibetans in many countries who needed *thangkas* to adorn family shrines. Each of them could complete a detailed *thangka* in about six weeks.

"Even if I get a chance to emigrate"—Genlak Tsering shook his head, looking at Thardoe, who would soon be departing from his instructional purview—"I will not take it. This is the best place for me to work." He mentioned the name of a fellow artist who had immigrated recently to Madison. That man now worked as a custodian, his years of rare, painstaking training useless in the new country.

We left the teacher's home studio and walked down shady streets to the institute, a modest two-story house, so Thardoe could say good-bye to his classmates. Shoes were piled at the entrance. Through an open window we could hear birds singing and the backfiring of a motorcycle. A couple dozen young men and one young woman sat barefooted and cross-legged on the floor, their canvases before them. Only the advanced students were allowed to paint. Beginning students used a compass and dissected the angles of Buddha's head or divided the paper to perfectly position lotus flowers in a composition. Genlak Tsering and Genlak Ngodup arrived in time for Thardoe's farewell lunch with his fellow students, for which Susan and I had purchased curries and sweets from a corner deli. Thardoe presented an envelope to Genlak Ngodup and gave another to Genlak Tsering as a donation to the school itself. Self-conscious, he gave a small speech of appreciation.

The single *thangka* he had finished, not something a first-year student was normally allowed to try, was striking in detail and artistry. I was disappointed he had chosen not to pursue the art form. I asked him why he had decided not to continue.

"My friends are back home in the US, and my parents don't think it's a real job," he said. "Only the best artists can make a living at this. And me, I get distracted. It would take so much focus and discipline." With those words, his year immersed in India's most famous Tibetan exile community, working under artists who held keys to a revered, disappearing art, came to an end. His grocery-bagging job awaited him back in Madison.

With Thardoe joining our departing entourage, my sister and I were escorted by not two but three young men, each one with his own brand of good looks—Tamdin's, like a movie star; Thardoe's, rugged; Namgyal's, a pleasant boy-next-door handsomeness. We took a last view of the magnificent mountain range that extended along India's border with former Tibet.

"I want to travel there at least once in my life," Thardoe said. Nearly all the Tibetan refugees I had met, whether born in Tibet or born in succeeding generations outside Tibet, said the same thing.

⌒

"India is a continent, not a country," people told Susan and me, referring to its vast size and almost incomprehensible diversity of people, politics, languages, landscapes, religions, and cuisine. Leaving Dharamsala, we traveled by bus, then long-distance train, then taxis, rickshaws, bicycles, and even long walks on dusty roads or hot, cracked sidewalks. In our total travels in India that month, we traveled farther than many Indians did in a lifetime, especially penurious people. Our senses vibrated with the intensity of colors, aromas, and pulsating rhythms.

India's 375,000 rail miles connect more cities and people than almost any other country in the world; only China's and Russia's rail lines outdistance them. Together the five of us returned to Delhi by bus for a brief check-in with Dickey's family. We purchased first-class tickets on the Rajadhani Express from Delhi in the state of Uttar Pradesh to Bengaluru (former Bangalore) in the state of Karnataka—all of us in high spirits at the prospect of three full, cross country travel days that lay ahead.

"This is not first class," grumbled Susan. The rest of us simply smiled. First class is a relative concept. In my previous trip to India, I once traveled third class for twelve hours in a train car so crowded that my nose smashed against the ceiling and the weight of my body was atop men below me. A few, in passing my horizontal body across the car, had "accidentally" placed a hand on my breast. It had been four hours before my feet finally touched the floor, as riders exited over a long series of jolting stops and starts. For those like me, wedged far from windows, passengers kindly bought and passed small, clay cups of tea. The car had been so jammed that my big pack had been torn from my shoulders and I figured it would be surely stolen. I was chagrined at my distrust when I eventually saw it lying in a corner, intact and untouched, and watched women disembark, gingerly lifting their skirts to step over its big splayed straps.

By contrast, on this Rajadhani Express we luxuriated in a near-private roomette that held the five of us plus one other passenger. At night a porter folded out beds from the walls so that we had triple bunks on each side. Namgyal, Tamdin, and Thardoe chattered away in Tibetan, delighted to be united after the year apart. Susan and I were enthralled by the cities and fields that streamed past. The tea seller appeared every hour or two, calling, "*Chai, chai, geram chai.*" ("Tea, tea, hot tea.") Serving men—never women, I noticed—appeared with adroitly balanced silver trays piled with saffron rice, potato *aloos*, spicy chicken *masalas*, pungent vegetable *biryanis*, dals, and more breads than I had known existed, *rotis*, naan, and *puris*. First class included meals.

All was to my liking until I took a break from the compartment and stood by an open train door. Slums and lean-tos hurtled past. A serving attendant appeared, lugging six black plastic garbage bags filled to the brim with passengers' crumpled paper plates and napkins, Styrofoam containers, and food scraps. He hurled them one by one out the open door, adding our rubbish to the knee-high wall of garbage that separated the rails from slums alongside. Small children ran to peek into the bags, and, as our train lumbered around a corner, I saw a small boy grab a sack twice his size and drag it toward a row of dilapidated tents.

～

This time it was not Tenzin's but Migmar's family who met us at the Bengaluru City railway station and shyly draped over the necks of each of us the long, white *khata*. Migmar's great-nephew, Norbu, had traveled with his wife six hours by local bus to meet our train. As honored guests, we would be treated to a shorter journey by cab, just five hours, from the station to the

Bylakuppe settlement where Tenzin, Migmar, and the kids had once lived and where Norbu's family still resided. We packed into the taxi with the Hindi-speaking driver, five people speaking Tibetan and two of us laughing right alongside, so infectious was the merriment and chatter. After we had been on the road only a matter of minutes, the driver pulled over at a Hindu shrine to buy a green plum. He held it before a priest, who sprinkled it with red powder to bless our journey. Off we went again, but not for long.

"Stop!" shouted Tamdin. "*Idli! Idli!*" Namgyal echoed him.

Idli are a staple of South India—hot rice flour pancakes served with coconut chutney and a steaming bowl of *saambaar* (lentil curry). The driver dutifully pulled over for our breakfast: stacks of *idli* accompanied by *vada*, pronounced "wada," a hot fried donut served with dipping sauces. As we sat at a small table, the boys' eyes looked dreamy, as if they were eating memories. Another thirty minutes down the road we pulled over again, this time to buy mangos from a roadside cart piled with pyramids of mangos, oranges, plums, and breadfruit. We bought ten mangos for twenty rupees—four cents each. Juices ran down our chins as we ate. A few kilometers farther on, we pulled off the road at another tiny eatery, this time for *thali*. *Thali* means "plate," but our "plate" was a banana leaf heaped with rice, dal, and small piles of sauces. I could name only one of them, yogurt.

Our companions concentrated on the food. No one bothered to sit together, no one waited for all to be served, and no one talked while eating. In Wisconsin, Tamdin had often gently criticized my attempts at making conversation during meals. "Tibetans talk after a meal," he would say, sidelining my what-did-you-do-at-school-today questions.

The roadside foliage was lush with crowds of tall papaya, banana, and coconut trees, hibiscus bushes in bloom beneath them, and orange orchards bent low with fruit. I, too, felt lush and heady, pregnant with the full joy of travel amidst the encompassing succulence. Namgyal, Tamdin, and Thardoe grew increasingly animated as we neared the childhood home they had left eight years earlier. The luxuriant greens changed to dense reds: redbrick houses that sat on red soil, and red-robed monks who walked at the side of the red-tinged asphalt road.

All three young men shouted victoriously as our car passed the gate that delineated the settlement's boundaries. We had arrived.

"What's different from when you left?" I asked them as we all looked from the windows of the taxi, bumping slowly over the gutted road.

"More traffic."

"More stores."

"New construction," they said, one after the other.

"New faces," Thardoe added. At this they all laughed. Our taxi had passed three lovely young women walking on the roadside.

"What's the same?" I asked them.

"Sugar cane fields, mangos, and *chupa*. And *lungi*," Tamdin answered exultantly. *Chupa* are Tibetan women's full-length dresses, and *lungi* are the wrap-around sarongs worn by men in South India, though not by Tibetan men.

Tamdin started pointing out to Susan and me all of his "places where."

"This is where we played hide-and-seek in the cornfields."

"This is where we chased one another around the community building."

"This is where we made plums into miniature cars and raced them down the road."

House No. 88, the house where the boys and their parents had lived, stood empty, but the brothers jumped out of the taxi so I could take a photo. In the Bylakuppe area alone, Old Camp 1 had been joined by five other original camps, in existence since 1962, plus fourteen new camps, each begun with about one hundred families. Three large temples and several monasteries and nunneries, with thousands of practicing monks and nuns, made Bylakuppe a major world magnet for Tibetan Buddhist study.

It was both awe-inspiring and heartbreaking to see what people who arrived in India with nothing had created in fifty years. The temples were spacious and golden, and donations had flowed in from practicing Buddhists in rich and poor nations the world over. The small homes, however, had cement floors, moldy walls, gunny sack ceilings, outdoor toilets, and common wells. Workers under the administration of the late Penor Rinpoche, one of Tibetan Buddhism's holy leaders, had paved temple roads, but the settlement streets were still dirt and potholed. The generous donations supported those who lived in the monastery complex, not the refugees who lived in the temple neighborhoods. Alighting from the taxi in front of House No. 85, where Migmar once lived with his brothers, we stepped around cow manure and the swishing tails of uncurious cows that blocked the road.

As others rushed out to greet us, a spry and slender white-haired woman, Aiji, ("Grandmother;" literally, "father's mother"), remained standing at the door, smiling and nodding. Soon we all stood before her. I could feel the intensity of respect others had for her and wished I knew the right expressions to say. Aiji had been a shared wife to three of Migmar's older brothers. One brother, her original husband, had died, and the other two took her in, not an uncommon practice in those days. One brother farmed; the other was, like Migmar, mostly away in the military. While the arrangement doubled the work and child-bearing expected of a woman, it had the advantage of keeping a family's precious land holdings under one roof. Aiji had been born in Tibet and thought she was about seventy-four. My language skills and our time together were inadequate to hear more details directly from her, but I hoped others might record what was surely a remarkable memoir.

Now I could see how Migmar's house connected with Tenzin's family's, immediately behind it. I saw the bamboo fence, chicken sheds, and makeshift stables for milking cows and goats. Tiny garden plots reigned in boisterous rows of bok choy, beans, peas, squash, and tomatoes. Vegetables, in the prime of summer heat, were to yield culinary ecstasy healthier than anything Susan and I ate back home.

It was not Aiji but men who were in her kitchen area. Acho (meaning "older brother") Gawa hummed as he diced, stirred, and shaped mutton and vegetarian *momo*, or dumplings, tandoori chicken, rice, dal, and other dishes in our honor, directing relatives who came in and out to help. I tried to jot down names and family relations, only to create notes filled with errors and misspellings. Namgyal, Tamdin, and Thardoe melted out of the house into the lively community, leaving Susan and me in the guest's role—to appreciate, ask, admire.

The brothers returned early the next day, which Susan and I later named Temple Day, as we were about to be escorted in and out of no fewer than four temples near the settlement. During my first trip to India almost twenty years earlier, my Muslim hosts took me to visit their neighborhood mosque immediately upon my arrival. In Japan, I had almost always been taken during my very first days to a nearby Shinto shrine or Buddhist temple, or both. Yet in the United States, I myself was more likely to take international visitors first to visit my friends or on a drive through affluent neighborhoods to see gentile mansions than to take anyone to my church, as if I even had one.

Entering the first temple, the Golden Temple of Namdroling Monastery, we took off our shoes. The brothers each prostrated themselves at least three times before the main Buddha statue. Namgyal touched his head to the *khata* he placed reverently at the statue's feet, and we left small donations of rupee notes atop the silk scarves.

One might study Buddhism for years in preparation to visit this ornate temple. A Buddhist might come for sightseeing, or to participate with hundreds of others in the ceremonies of prayers and *pujas* of the monastic community, or to study in the *shadra* (Buddhist college) or three-year retreat center. Four thousand monks and one thousand nuns trained here in logic, philosophy, debate, and doctrinal systems. Of the four major schools of Tibetan Buddhism, this monastery belonged to the Nyingma School. The Dalai Lama was trained mainly in the Gelug School, but he occasionally gave teachings from the Nyingma lineage, as well as from the other two main schools, Kagyu and Sakya.

I had been dropped here, like an eagle drops a mouse, awed to find myself not only in such a majestic building but amidst a layered, reverent world. Outside, breezes blew through the sandalwood grove, and the peaceful, meditative calm distanced the clatter of wheels. The eighteen-meter-high, gold-leafed Buddha stared down at us, as if he were unimpressed with the piles of scarves and fruits and human attempts at compassion and wisdom.

Leaving Namdroling, we passed young monks sitting on the formal garden lawn in front of a sign that read, in English, "Do not sit on grass." They were drinking Coke and Sprite.

Pilgrim tourism brought tens of thousands of visitors each year to the temples and settlements. It had become necessary to require visitors to apply and register, and I kept seeing signs that all visitors needed a Protective Area Permit (PAP) to stay overnight. Perhaps our Tibetan friends had not read the tourist guidebooks, or perhaps they had already registered Susan and me. I was again aware of walking a path of insider privilege, gazing upon this remarkable, historical site, holy to 350 million of the world's practicing Buddhists.

Would the original settlers, the ones like Migmar's brothers who hacked away the tropical jungles and suffered tiger attacks, imagine that the overgrown forests would become, in just five decades, a sacred, protected area, teeming with curious travelers and reverent believers?

"Now we're going to the Dalai Lama's main temple," Tamdin said with pride. On our way he tried to explain to Susan and me the differences among the four main lineages of Tibetan Buddhism: which scriptures were taught, how one meditated, and different terms the practitioners used. He told us that all Tibetan Buddhist schools and traditions of practice can trace their origin directly back to the original Buddha Sakyamuni, born in 563 BCE in what is now Nepal. Each school of Tibetan Buddhism traces its founding in Tibet to a particular person, who in turn was connected to a particular tradition in India. It was a mind-bending topic, better suited to a university course on world religions. Even if I didn't fully understand, I admired Tamdin's fearless plunge into deep waters of monastic nuance.

Down the road, our destination, the Sera Monastery complex, consisted of Sera Mey and Sera Jay colleges for three thousand monks and a Great Assembly Hall. Sera Jey was short for Sera Jey Monastic University for Advanced Buddhist Studies and Practice, and Sera May, similarly, was Sera May Theosam Norling School, Deemed University for Advanced Buddhist Studies and Practice. The colleges bestowed the equivalent of master's (Geshe) and PhD (Lharam Geshe) degrees in philosophy, the first involving study spanning nineteen years, the latter an additional six years, both including debate, memorization, analysis of texts, meditation, prayers, and living in a monastic setting of "loving kindness, compassion, wisdom and the pursuit of ultimate reality," according to the brochure. The Namdroling complex grounds included a primary school, secondary school, health care facility, food-service kitchens, a social service building, and water purification plant. Both were sister or replacement monasteries to gigantic, ancient temples in Tibet proper that were either destroyed when the Chinese invaded or inaccessible to Tibetan refugees, or both. These were worlds within worlds.

Compared to the Namdroling temple, Sera Monastery's temple, named Sera Lachi, appeared more modest and worn. Several times during the day, when we had happened upon a locked building, one of the brothers would dart off to return with a monk or caretaker, key in hand, seemingly pleased to open these treasures of faith to curious foreigners. There were rooms in each of the temple-monastery complexes reserved specifically for the occasional visits from His Holiness. At one point, the brothers politely asked a kind caretaker if we could see His Holiness the Dalai Lama's sitting room, which led us to the Dalai Lama's press room, and the Dalai Lama's bedroom. I peeked into the Dalai Lama's refrigerator.

Exhausted after still more temples, Susan and I sighed gratefully when the brothers turned back toward the settlement about sunset. For every hour we had been gone, Acho Gawa had created yet another sumptuous dish. For a single meal, he had summoned from the gardens and grounds spicy tandoori chicken and mutton; spinach, cucumbers, tomatoes, and bok choy; a mouthwatering and smooth *paneer* made of blended Indian cheese and *ghee*; the now-familiar *tukpa* noodle soup; butter-fried *chapati*; homemade yogurt; and, as if we needed more, a sweet custard and *gulab jamun*—delectable honey-soaked pastry balls—to top it off. We all ate as if we had spent the afternoon ascending Everest. Acho Gawa grinned with satisfaction.

❧

Our days around the settlement gave colors, aromas, and textures to the stories that Tenzin, Migmar, and the children had told me during the previous eight years. We visited the brothers' former primary school, where quiet, respectful students sat in straight rows of desks. I remembered the children's unhappiness when they first encountered the noisier, more interactive US classrooms. We heard a class of thirty-six students learning English recite a string of verbs in droning unison: "Run, running, eat, eating," et cetera. Tamdin recalled that he had memorized his classroom English in the small elementary school, seldom with any idea what English words meant. In third grade, he remembered answering test questions following a story. "Where did Ramalinga live?" was one question, and Tamdin obediently parroted back, "He lived in the kingdom of Vijay Nager." But he had no comprehension of what the words meant, much less any sense of the history of India's great nineteenth-century Tamil saint, poet, and opponent to the caste system.

We talked to math and history teachers at the school who told us their salaries, less than one thousand dollars per month, were twice that of teachers at the neighboring TCV School, which took in orphaned children, but five times less than they could earn as high-tech workers in India's cosmopolitan centers.

❧

I didn't immediately notice that Thardoe, the youngest brother, the one who had been studying in India all year, the one who had already been to Bylakuppe several times to visit relatives and to take his grandfather to Kalachakra, was often absent. He was hoping no one would notice that he was spending time with his girlfriend, Samkyi, a young woman he had known in his childhood days in the settlement. In the interconnected web of Tibetan acquaintances, Samkyi, here in the south, was the cousin of Lhakpa, Namgyal's new girlfriend up north, whom Namgyal was telephoning each night as we continued our travels. The brothers' barbs to Thardoe and the elders' sly references had undoubtedly gone right over my head. Susan and I seemed the last to catch on we had a third romance in our midst.

Leaving Thardoe in Bylakuppe to his romantic exploits, after an awkward reminder to him about the dangers of HIV and STDs, my sister Susan and I split off from our adopted Tibetan families for several days. I wanted her to feel the flavors of India outside of refugee settlements. From Mysore, Susan and I traveled by bus to Matakeri. However, as soon as we stopped there to switch buses, we were approached by small boys selling flutes, older boys selling locusts, a toothless man hawking watches, and several touts who rushed to help us find a "good hotel, not expensive." I wondered how to part from the unwelcome attention, but Susan, in a burst of magnanimity, gave rupees to a wrinkled elderly woman and a package of biscuits to a thin, old man. The crowd around us pressed closer. A lovely young woman in a sari stepped in and asked in English if she could help. She gracefully shooed away the crowd and guided us to our correct bus. How protected we had been, in the past weeks, traveling with the three brothers.

The roads from Matakeri gave way to lush, wet, tropical jungles of blossoming cardamom, ginger, guava, and jackfruit trees. We entered former English hill station country, the old forts and Raj estates of British millionaire coffee owners replaced by the neocolonialism of Indian millionaires. We walked down roads through quiet plantations and met workers who told us they made 130 rupees a day ($2.60 in those years). The equivalent of a pound of coffee beans sold in shops for 60 rupees ($1.20) back then, compared to $7.20 per pound in Madison stores, the 700 percent markup a study in global market middlemen.

In a rickshaw, we visited Ranganathittu Bird Sanctuary, awed by cormorants, storks, spoonbills, and kingfishers. Back in Mysore on our circle tour, we climbed three hundred steps up Chamundi Hill to Sri Chamundeshwari Hindu Temple, where dark-skinned women sold sandalwood incense and wreaths of marigolds to long lines of worshippers in rainbow-colored saris—a virtual kaleidoscope of India's many faces.

Any tourist could visit bird sanctuaries and Hindu temples, but we no longer had our own personal guides to the culture. We had traveled in a Tibetan bubble, shielded from those who are drawn to foreign tourists, but also separated from and learning nothing about India's disparate Hindus, Jains, Sikhs, and Muslims, or meeting any Punjabi-, Kannadan-, Tamil-, and Telegu-speaking people.

Jarred by how quickly our journey had transitioned to mere tourism, we reconnected in the city of Bengaluru with just two brothers, Namgyal and Tamdin, to return for our third and last pass through Delhi. Thardoe had decided to stay longer in Byla-kuppe, a sure sign that the attraction was growing more serious. In Bengaluru's small airport, we spotted Namgyal and Tamdin amidst an entire entourage of our settlement hosts—uncles, aunts, nephews, in-laws and cousins, all except Aiji. Everyone had started at 7 a.m. and traveled six hours by bus to the airport just to see us off, before journeying six hours back. The brothers wore silver necklaces, gifts from Acho Gawa. The triumphant return to their boyhood home shone in their faces. Relatives draped so many *khata* around our necks that our eyes disappeared in white, silken circles.

By air, four of us—Susan, Namgyal, Tamdin, and I— recrossed the route south to north, Bengaluru to Delhi, in two and a half hours, the same route that had taken us thirty-six hours by train, more than two thousand miles, roughly the distance from Chicago to San Francisco. I looked down to see tiny Indian villages surrounded by hundreds of patchwork fields, a completely different landscape from the midwestern pattern of barn and field and farmhouse. Villagers walked long distances to plant and harvest those fields—their feet, hoes, and back-breaking labor a substitute for midwestern trucks, tractors, and threshers. As in the United States, I imagined the country's huge, still-undeveloped tracks of green were shrinking year by year. As we approached Delhi, the tiny dots of houses grew thicker, like a completed jigsaw puzzle, finally becoming one burnished mass. Even from the air, the rivers looked dirty. And after the clear, cool days in Mysore, Delhi's heat seemed oppressive.

To get to Dickey's house for our remaining days in India, we again veered into the melee of traffic. All fought for space in jammed lanes—bicycles and auto rickshaws pressed alongside limos with windows closed and dirt-matted buses with windows open and men hanging out from the doors, unafraid to meet my gaze. At stoplights, small girls knocked on our windows to sell flower garlands woven of lotus, jasmine, and trumpet flowers. I worried about the safety of these tiny figures darting into and out of traffic, as they earned money for their families. Would the garlands, blessings for Hindu *puja* worship, protect them from the angry onrush of men and machines?

With eight of us at the table, including Rajid, the twelve-year-old servant, our final dinner at Dickey's house was merry. I was happy to have Rajid sitting with us, instead of serving us. He was a curious and charming boy, one of millions of Indian children who did not attend school. The Tibetan family in Delhi, like many Indian families, prided themselves on rescuing these children from abject poverty and providing them food, housing, and clothes. Dickey's family seemed glad to be able to afford servants, far from the days when her and Tenzin's mother and

father, Pema Choedon and Tsewang Paldon, had hewn a settlement with bare hands. Social service agencies in India nonetheless waged campaigns to wean families from using children as
servants and urged them to enroll these small girls and boys in
school. A youth of servitude only prepared a child for an adulthood of the same.

～

The three brothers would linger in India another month, but
Susan and I packed for our flight back to Wisconsin. Susan was
looking forward to drinking steaming hot Starbucks coffee
from a paper cup, unlike the sweet, lukewarm coffee in plastic
cups, and I was nervous to see if my Peace Corps assignment
had arrived in my Madison mailbox. Just as the Bylakuppe
relatives had done, Dickey and her family gathered en masse on
the cracked sidewalk on an avenue bustling with cars and buses.
I stepped over dog feces that no one ever seemed to pick up, and
ignored an old man asleep on a cot by a puddle of rain. A taxi
driver spotted us, affluent-looking passengers, and braked with
a screech, splashing water on the sleeping man.

To step over the puddle from the curb, I had to stretch my leg
into the cab. It was a huge step. It was the I-am-going-to-the-
international-airport step, the step between the haves and have-
nots of the world. It was the step that separates those who have
the luxury to wander between the world's pockets of prosperity
and poverty, from those whose sphere is confined to a smaller
circumference. That bittersweet step marks my greatest wealth.

～

On the plane back to Chicago, I looked down on the borders of
Kashmir, Pakistan, and Afghanistan, lit with military strobes
in the black night. As usual, I was one of few passengers who
kept her nose pressed against the windows almost the entire

flight. Impressions of the past weeks pulsated as the plane's lights blinked in the remote skies.

Throughout our trip, I had felt my Tibetan family's presence in places far from Wisconsin. The families I met, all connected to the one in Madison, touched my life and held me in theirs, the line between sky and ocean no longer discernible. I had been startled that new immigrants who seemed to have very little in the United States retained deep ties to their ancient culture and held the keys to admit me to monasteries, temples, and settlements I could not have entered alone. I had been surprised that I had a reputation among people I had never met, that the unremarkable kindnesses I had extended had reverberated across an ocean. I had felt the peace and mystery of Buddhism in the country that had given birth to three of the world's great religions.

In contrast, I had also been haunted by the immense piles of garbage and alarmed at India's lack of infrastructure and land-use planning. I had been saddened by the illiteracy of young Indians. I had been dismayed at how the world, and I myself, managed to step over or around abject poverty, leaving it unchanged.

This trip, thanks to Tenzin, renewed my appreciation for what lay nearest. In this adventure with a family that was not my biological family, I had been given a rare chance to be together night and day with my sister Susan. I loved her willingness to venture in spaces of discomfort and to tolerate my way of travel, so different from hers—to engage with strangers on trains and on the street, to venture off established paths, to stay in homes and monasteries rather than bed-and-breakfast suites. I was touched how my Tibetan family welcomed her with affection. When Tenzin said "family," she didn't mean just her own.

How do we decide who is our family? What experiences allow us to draw others into our innermost orbits of love and trust? As my Tibetan family had expanded, I had become nearer to my Oklahoma family as well.

Our plane from India to Chicago was hours late to arrive, which delayed our bus ride to Madison. Migmar and Tenzin took a day without pay away from their jobs to meet Susan and me. They stretched out their arms and put *khata* around our necks. Still dizzy from the transatlantic buzz separating my Wisconsin home from my new families in Delhi, Dharamsala, and Bylakuppe, I gave them big hugs. Susan and I put small gifts from Tenzin's family in India into Tenzin's hands, as precious for the love they embodied as for their aromas of sandalwood, silk, and patchouli. I didn't need to mention anything about the romances in process. Transatlantic emails had beat me to it.

"*Tashi delek. Tashi delek*," they greeted us. "Welcome home."

CHAPTER 10

Tangled Traditions

*Culture is a seashell where we hear voices of what we are,
what we were, what we forget, and what we can be.*
—CARLOS FUENTES, MEXICAN AUTHOR

Our trip to India, where Tibetan traditions seemed well integrated into daily life in the settlements, made me curious to look
more closely at the same traditions back home in Madison. For
my Tibetan American family, the move to the United States
diluted or erased some customs but changed and expanded
others. Migmar and Tenzin had stuffed their duffel bags with
clothes and small Buddha icons, but what about the invisible
baggage they had carried? What cultural practices lived on in
my family's house on Midvale Boulevard?

When I would come to visit, I would sometimes encounter
Migmar and Tenzin roasting barley, called *tsampa*, on their
front porch, squatting before a gas-fueled burner. Like many
Asians, they slipped off their shoes when going inside the house,
acknowledging the barrier between the outer, polluted world and
the inner one of peace and sanctity. Migmar and Tenzin frequently sat right down on their carpeted kitchen floor to pound
whole seeds of mustard, allspice, cumin, anise, and nutmeg in
a large brass mortar. The entire family might sit cross-legged on

a sheet spread out on the living room floor, able to turn out one hundred *momo* in a single hour, each person speedily creating exact, perfect rounds or half-moon patterns. If I stopped by when this dumpling making was in process, their pace would slow, and with tolerant smiles, like one assumes when teaching a child how to tie her shoes, they would show me the patterns, yet again.

A "Free Tibet" yard sign or a colorful string of prayer flags attached to a tree branch were clues to a home where a Tibetan American family might reside. Inside most of these homes, visitors would find a family shrine. I would catch my breath in awe at the colors and elaborate figurines when I entered the room that housed my family's shrine, called a *choesham*. Whether the shrine was in the corner of a modern home in Wisconsin or in the stucco houses I had visited in the Indian settlements, the white, orange, yellow, and red of the ribbons, the soft beauty of burning candles, and the earthy, herbal fragrance of incense beckoned me into its mystical space.

When I asked about the family altar, Migmar pointed out how the three shelves of a Tibetan Buddhist altar had specific functions: something that symbolized the scriptures, from which all Buddhist teachings can be traced, was on the top shelf; items representing one's religious teachers were found on the second tier; and offerings were presented on the bottom shelf. Offerings varied by the day and season. They might be flowers, fruits, lit candles, or incense. The *thangka* that Thardoe had painted in India had its place among the family's growing collection, hanging on walls near the shrine.

On the top level of my family's shrine were not only a small, gold statue of the Buddha but also figurines of other ancient gods that were family heirlooms. After we returned from India, I stood in front of them, wondering if some had been carried all the way from Tibet. I studied the gold-framed photographs of

His Holiness and a tiny replica of his 1989 Nobel Peace Prize on the second shelf, draped with gold-colored ceremonial *khata*, signifying purity and compassion.

Migmar told me it was less important what objects were on the shelves than that each object had been chosen with a sense of compassion and generous heart. Though the items looked ornate to me, Migmar said that inexpensive, simple objects were fine, even preferable. The Buddha, like Jesus, had renounced material wealth and found wisdom through simplicity, but Migmar did not say this. He was teaching me basic principles of Buddhism in his casual, unassuming manner.

On the lowest level, seven silver offering cups, evenly spaced "the length of a grain of rice apart," were filled to the exact same level with water or rice. Each cup symbolized attributes to which one aspires, like purity of heart, generosity, and discipline. Migmar refilled these cups early in the morning, always from left to right. In the late afternoon, to empty them, he reversed the order, putting the old water to use on indoor plants.

For him, the shrine was a place for meditation, day after day, month after month, year after year. Like the great shrines and stupas to which others made pilgrimage to honor sites where the Buddha and other great teachers had prayed and practiced, the family shrine achieved its sacredness through daily attention and practice. It was where individuals cultivated the enlightened mind, let loose of troubling habits, and dedicated their actions to helping others.

"Have you ever met the Dalai Lama?" I had asked the children in their first year in Madison.

"Oh, lots of times," Thardoe assured me. "He visited our school in India all the time."

When His Holiness came to town, which he did on numerous occasions, Madisonians were excited and near worshipful. Each time, while I merely bought a ticket and sat amidst thousands of people to listen to him, my family went into high gear. They attended invariably packed, specially organized Wisconsin Tibetan Association meetings with him, conducted in Tibetan. They joined security units to escort and guard him 24-7, cooked for the retinue of monks and dignitaries that accompanied him, and attended special observances at Deer Park. In the children's eyes, he was not only an esteemed leader, but a dear, approachable, avuncular friend. They felt they knew him, and by the way he smiled at them each time he passed through their midst, they were certain he recognized them.

～

I tried to create American Thanksgiving and Christmas holiday traditions with Tenzin's family when they arrived in the United States—days they referred to as "Madeline's holidays." As a single person, I received invitations to holiday dinners at friends' homes, and in the years before her family arrived, I often brought Tenzin along with me.

When Migmar and the children settled in, I longed to introduce them to my friends' lavish, multicourse repasts—not only the traditional turkey, gravy, cranberries, and pumpkin pie— but roasted goose with wild rice stuffing, berry compotes, and multilayer tortes beneath mounds of whipped cream.

"Is it okay if I bring guests?" I asked.

"Sure!" my friends replied. "Will Tenzin be coming with you again?"

"Her family arrived. How about seven of us?" I asked, my voice escalating an octave.

"Well," my friends said, "maybe not." We laughed politely on both ends of the telephone.

So I was on my own.

Our holiday feasts became strange amalgamations of their and my favorite foods—turkey, shrimp, and pickled herring on my part, and *momo*, *tukpa*, and curried vegetables on theirs—neither traditionally American nor traditionally Indo-Tibetan, but uniquely "us." Like immigrants before them, my adopted family became active players in the death, rebirth, and reconstruction of ethnic traditions in their new country.

"Let's each say what we are thankful for," I would suggest as we gathered for Thanksgiving. As we clinked our glasses in a toast, then held hands around the table, they all giggled in embarrassment, hesitated at length, and invariably contributed single words. "You, Madeline." "Everybody." "Friends." Migmar raised a plate of food and murmured a Buddhist prayer.

In my Oklahoma family, we five kids had bowed to our parents' encouragement that we create stories or plays as our gifts to them. At Folklore Village, where I had worked in my twenties and thirties, I had helped with that folk art center's Mid-Winter Festivals—elaborate, four- and five-day re-creations of solstice, Jewish, Christian, and Orthodox Christian practices from many countries. During my year in Dalarna, Sweden, I had been enchanted by Jul celebrations that involved candlelit churches, horse-drawn sleighs over deep snow, Santa Lucia with candles in her hair, and torches lit along the winding river. Religion played little part in my celebrations, though a yearning for the combination of candles and carols sometimes drew me to midnight masses in churches where I never set foot otherwise. Like the gnome-ish Swedish *tomptar*, I deemed Christmas a magical, rather than sacred, season, and I was determined to re-create the wonder and sparkle with Tenzin's family. Just as I had no way of knowing how Tibetan traditions were practiced from one family or village to another, they had no way of knowing that "Madeline's holidays" were imaginative mélanges quite different from any neighbors.'

Every winter, a couple of weeks before December 25, I would begin hunting for my stockings, cookie cutters, and Swedish

Julgran candle holders and would pile pillows, brooms, and music CDs for skits, games, and folk dances in which I imagined we would lightheartedly engage. The boys and I would tromp in the snow to cut-your-own tree stands to choose a small, always imperfect—since it had to be inexpensive—Norway pine. Because it would bear candles, it needed to be fresh and have widely spaced branches.

Santa Claus appeared each Christmas, but he was a Santa unlike those seen in other American homes. Our Santa, played by a rotating cast of the three brothers, was always howling with laughter or doubled over with giggles, wearing all-red clothing I had set out on an upstairs bed—my red Japanese *hanten* jacket, my red bathrobe, my red turtleneck, and a beard that Santa and his helper would quickly construct from Scotch tape and cotton balls, a veritable modern art oddity on Santa's chin. Downstairs I would be making gravy or dishing up dessert. I never took time to dress Santa properly. Besides, his entrance was supposed to be a surprise, and it was my task to keep the others distracted while Santa was dressing.

One year when Kunsel, a young nephew of theirs, burst into tears at Santa's appearance, Namgyal, who was playing the jolly old elf, ripped off his mask, surprising both me and the baby. I hoped that Kunsel's psychic wounds would heal, but after that I became nervous Santa might suddenly disrobe, mid-role.

For the teens' first Christmas in Madison, I planned to follow my anti-materialistic inclinations and establish a family custom of a holiday without gifts. My idea was to show them other splendid traditions of the season—sledding, decorating cookies, and lighting real candles on a tree. At the office, however, my colleagues frowned when I told them my plan. Two days before Christmas, they presented me with four hundred dollars in cash they had collected among themselves.

They beamed. "This is for gifts for your new family."

My heart sank. In hindsight I wish I had given the cash to Tenzin and Migmar, but instead I doggedly fought through frantic crowds of last-minute shoppers and bought pairs of in-line skates for the kids, in sizes I wasn't sure would fit. For Tenzin and Migmar I raced around to find inexpensive gifts, fuming the whole time amidst the seasonal bedlam.

On that December 25, nine people, the six of them plus Tenzin's niece Karma and her two children, walked through my door, each bearing a gift—nine gifts, all for me. "Merry Christmas, Madeline. Merry Christmas!" Each of them unwrapped one gift from me and then watched patiently and proudly for more than an hour as I unwrapped nine brand-new, relatively expensive sweaters, jackets, and kitchen utensils. I tried to hide my sense of failure, as it was obvious by their huge smiles that they had, despite me, discovered the joy and generosity of Christmas in the United States—store-bought Christmas presents.

"Thank you, Namgyal. Thank you, Tamdin, I'll use this a lot. Thank you, Tenzin, it's very pretty." Among my gifts was a plug-in waterfall that created a corner for peaceful meditation. It murmured tranquilly behind my toppling pile of acquisitions.

"Let's sing Christmas carols," I suggested after the unwrapping ordeal came to a close, determined to share other traditions. "Do you know 'Silent Night'?" The children, all in Madison's public schools, nodded yes. So I started singing, "Silent night, holy night . . ." Everyone nodded encouragingly. My friends refer to my singing voice as loud and tuneless, and this was, I believe, my only public solo ever. At the end of my performance, trying to act as if a monotone solo was part of every family's Christmas, I said, "Now you sing a song, any song." They laughed self-consciously.

"We don't do Christmas," Namgyal said, stating the obvious.

"But, you sing," I insisted. They demurred politely. Maybe

they sang while they danced, or maybe they chanted prayers, or maybe they had sung planting songs in the fields of the settlement back in India. But no one could think of a single song to sing under Madeline's Christmas tree.

Their family included many people, and I had enjoyed delightful customs in their home. I was just one person, however, and when I tried to create a whole holiday, I felt the challenge of defining, isolating, and displaying my culture, suddenly out of focus and context.

᠆᠊᠎

Tenzin and Migmar got Thanksgiving Day, Christmas Day, and Labor Day off work as holidays, but unless I invited them to my house, these became days when they would watch football and basketball games on TV or catch up on sleep. No turkeys appeared for roasting or trees for decorating. They did, however, quickly discover that American holidays merited time-and-a-half pay, so among their coworkers, they became popular for their willingness to work these extra shifts. For their own New Year's celebration later in the winter, as well as for Tibetan Uprising Day on March 10, the Dalai Lama's birthday on July 6, Democracy Day on September 2, or the month in which Saka Dawa (Buddha's birth, enlightenment, and death) fell, usually in the springtime as determined by the Tibetan calendar, they had to request permission to take off workdays without pay.

᠆᠊᠎

Tenzin's family's year began with their own primary holiday, Tibetan New Year, called *Losar*. The dates, often in February or March but different each year, were announced annually by His Holiness the Dalai Lama based on ancient calculations. *Losar* predates Buddhism and can be traced to ancient times when farmers offered blessings for successful crops and good fortune to spirits that existed beneath each rock, within the flowing waters of rivers and springs, and atop every mountain. Throughout Tibet, Bhutan, Nepal, India, and other countries, modern-day *Losar* has combined the sacred and the secular, and today's Tibetans in exile communities mix ancient ceremonies, prayers, and the hanging of new prayer flags, with dancing—whether religious, folk, or disco—in successive days of celebrating. It started even before New Year's.

"Come to dinner tonight. We'll have *guthuk*, New Year's Eve soup," Tenzin said to me one February. When I arrived, the weather outside cold and overcast, I found her and Lhadon still scrubbing and vacuuming, their hair protected from flying dust with kerchiefs. Migmar had returned from a giant shopping trip and was in the kitchen, filling all the rice, spice, and tea leaf containers to the brim for a fresh start on the year's cooking. New clothes and new sheets and new dish cloths peeked from unopened shopping bags.

Moving to the sparkling-clean kitchen, Tenzin introduced me to *guthuk*, a noodle soup full of dumplings. The *gu-* in *guthuk* (and in *Gutar*, the two days of cleaning preceding *Losar*) means "nine," and I watched as she pulled out nine ingredients to start the soup, including meat, dried cheese, and green beans, plus flour for the dumplings. She put something small into some of the wads of dumpling dough—a small piece of "coal" (actually a black bean) in one, a piece of thread in another, or a slice of chili pepper, a scrap of cotton, or a scrap of paper. On the papers she wrote words in Tibetan, meaning "sun," "moon," "salt," or "glass." Each tiny object represented an attribute of personality, like *karyul*, meaning "glass," for a person who's only around when times are good, or *nyima*, meaning "sun," for a person with a sunny personality.

That night at dinner, the children tentatively bit into their dumplings, and laughter and teasing erupted when they first tasted one containing an odd item.

"Lhadon! You have a bad heart!" Lhadon had bitten into the "coal."

"Migmar! That's the cotton. You have a kind heart!" Migmar scooped a tiny cotton wad out of his mouth with a finger.

I had bitten into a bit of red pepper, and everyone laughed knowingly. "Talkative! Sharp tongue!"

From a lump of leftover noodle dough, into which we pressed a thread from our clothes, we made a small person, called a *dhre-jang*, or *lue*, to carry all the bad luck from the house. We passed the *dhre-jang* around our body, three times to the right, then three times to the left.

"Now, touch it to your body parts that hurt," Tenzin instructed me and tapped the dough effigy to her fingers, back, ankles—all currently aching. Migmar, who was losing teeth, touched his to his mouth. We put our figurines into the serving bowl and added our leftovers.

"In Tibet, we added soot from the mud stove," Migmar told me, through someone's translation.

"Make a wish for the new year, and pour out nine drops. You won't have bad luck this year," Tenzin promised.

When I had lived in Japan, Buddhist temple gongs rang 108 times on New Year's Eve, to rid families, communities, and the world of 108 types of misfortune. In Tibetan Buddhism, there were 81 bad omens (*teh ngen*), and both numbers, 81 and 108, are multiples of 9. Somewhere there was undoubtedly a list of them all—greed, lust, thievery, violence, judgment, envy, hunger for power and wealth. Not only I, but the entire world, needed more of these humbling ceremonies for casting out demons of unhappiness and reclaiming our pure hearts and intentions.

In Tibet, Migmar told us, one of the women from each household would take these dregs of bad luck from the house to dump in the bushes. After giving her a head start, one man from each family jumped up, lit a torch, and went to search for her in the snowy darkness, calling out three times, *"Bamo dhon shoma!"* ("Witches, get out!") Meanwhile, family members went from room to room, shouting three times in each room, *"Bama dhon shoma!"*

Migmar laughed, his eyes crinkled with mischief, as he called out the Tibetan phrase. The mirthful women would scurry to a hiding place they had chosen ahead of time, while the men, finding no one, would light a bush or brush pile on fire to scare away remaining demons, or fire guns into the night air. Today in diaspora settlements in India, fireworks replace the noisy, torch-lit search. In Madison, someone would dump the *guthuk* noodles at the busy intersection outside, according to superstition, to confuse the evil spirits that come looking for family members. In later years, the noodles were simply deposited in the dumpster.

With their home spotless and its bad spirits banished, Tenzin's family welcomes in their new year. For example, 2015 was year 2142 on the Tibetan calendar, or the Year of the Wood Sheep. Similar to the Chinese Zodiac, Tibetans combine the order of twelve animal signs with the five elements—fire, earth, iron, water, and wood—in a complex way that demarks sixty-year cycles. In earlier times, the New Year celebrations lasted fifteen days, and each day had prescribed activities. Even today in rural Tibet, families might celebrate for five days. In their Indian settlement, my family had celebrated for three days, so this is what they did in Madison.

The first day of the Tibetan New Year, always beginning on a new moon, is propitious and religious, designated for prayers and blessings. In 2015, as in other years, throngs of Madison's Tibetans and their friends, most in full traditional dress, drove to Deer Park Buddhist Center, fondly called "the jewel in the heartland of America," amidst country fields outside Oregon, Wisconsin. The winter sun glistened off the auspicious symbols and medallions atop the roof—deer and wheel, victory spires and lotus spire, hand-crafted by artisans in India.

Inside, hundreds of men, women, and children arranged themselves gracefully atop rows of burgundy-colored floor cushions. I was relieved to see older people sitting in chairs along the sides of the ornate temple room, with its high ceilings and wood-paneled walls from which hung dozens of long *thangka*. I snagged an empty chair. At a blast of horns and drums, a line of monks in long robes and high hats entered the room. The congregants began chanting a prayer, reading from Tibetan script. A woman tiptoed over to me and placed in my lap a prayer book translated into English. But which prayer were we doing? The older man beside me, who I later learned was an esteemed emeritus professor of Tibetan studies, leaned over to point to a line. Those who understood Tibetan and those who were students of Buddhism were reading the sixteen Arhats, special prayers that ask for the long life of spiritual teachers, for peace on earth, for harmony in the hearts of men and women, and for auspiciousness for all in the coming year.

Already several weeks before this service, Tenzin and her children had baked *khapse*, curled and fried sweet pastries, which Migmar piled in elaborate, crisscrossed stacks on the family shrine in preparation for New Year's. Each shape had its own name: donkey ears (*bhungue amcho* or *khugo*), braids (*mukdung*), and knots (*kongchen*). The recipes were regional, the techniques for Losar altar artistry were centuries-old, and Migmar's design sense shone. Before decorating the shrine, he carefully placed the first piece of *kapse*, called a scorpion, to the side of the stove, to remain there all the days of Losar, its job to ward off kitchen burns and spills and other bad luck. In his boyhood in Tibet, Migmar remembers people drawing a scorpion shape with their finger on the wall, using soot from the cooking circle, to honor the spirit of the stove. It remained there all year.

Everything the first day of the New Year's celebration was done with careful consciousness of first encounters with the five sacred elements. Migmar consciously noted the first rays of sunrise, striking his first match to light the first incense, turning on the tap to run the first water for the first tea. Blessing his family, Migmar brought first cups of steaming tea on a tray to his still-sleeping wife and children. In India, Tenzin told me, the eight water taps at the refugee village were tied with white *khata*. On these New Year's mornings in Wisconsin, Migmar tied a scarf above the faucet, just as his own grandmother had once tied a scarf at a spring seeping from the mountainside.

On the third day of the New Year, *Losar* parties and visiting began in earnest. Tibetan American friends would greet their hosts with, "*Tashi delek.*" Even before removing their coats and gloves, they would go to the family shrine where they would take a pinch of *chemar* from the right side of a beautifully carved wooden box called the *chemar bo*. In Tibet, roasted barley grains are used to make *chemar*, though wheat is used in the United States, mixed with sugar and butter. The visitors would then recite:

Tashi Delek PhunSoom Tsok,
Ama BhakDro KunKham Zhang,
Ten Dhu Dewa Thopar Shok,
Dusang Tukyi Tatseo Yanggyar Zomgyu Yongwa Sho.

(With a pure mind, heart and body,
I pray for blessing and good luck,
and wish for the good health of mothers.
May all beings become enlightened
and may we all be here next year to celebrate together.)

While reciting the blessing, they would wave the tiny grains three times and then toss them gently in the air, before reaching into the box again to take a small pinch of the powdery barley flour from the left side to touch to their tongues.

My family's New Year's shrine was as magical as any Christmas tree. Candles flickered, the air filled with incense, and the shrine, expanded to a table, overflowed with *khata*-draped piles of *kapse*, wrapped candies, and bottles of whisky and home-brewed *chang* (rice wine). Migmar murmured blessings not only for his family, but for all the world's peoples, not only for those living, but for those recently and long deceased.

Each year, somewhere amidst the days of parties with their Tibetan American friends and the large community-wide gatherings feted by the Wisconsin Tibetan Association, Tenzin and Migmar hosted a gala New Year's party in their home, welcoming their non-Tibetan friends: me, Migmar's English teacher Shoko, and work colleagues and residents from Kennedy Manor. As we arrived, we each did the barley and *chemar* blessing at the altar, stumbling over the words in the blessing, repeating phrases as one of the teens would say them first. Year after year, "*Tashi Delek PhunSoom Tsok*" was as far as I could get.

Raised in an Oklahoma Unitarian family whose values defied our Bible Belt setting, I stood before the *chemar bo* and felt connected to the ancient Tibetan words. Was I not one of the earth's people? Was it not my duty to honor living things, to have courage to stand against hatred and prejudice, and to nurture those younger than me? Yes, blessings on all the world's mothers. Blessings upon this family who so unassumingly shared their lives with me. I hoped we would all be here together in a year. What finer wish for the new year could there be?

The other guests often peppered my family with questions about New Year's traditions in Tibet, just as I was always doing.

"Why do you do that? What is this called? What's the name of this food?"

We non-Tibetan guests socialized in the living room, speaking English, while our hosts bustled in and out of the kitchen, speaking Tibetan, bringing more drinks and snacks and eventually a full, steaming meal. Socializing at a party is language- and culture-specific. I felt awkward, wishing for a game or song to bring us together into one room.

"Isn't there a game we can play?" I asked.

"Yes," one would answer, "but you need to speak Tibetan to play it."

Then one *Losar*, Samkyi, who by now had become Thardoe's wife, sang a hauntingly sad song called "*Rigshengi Metok.*" At first, I imagined it was about one lover pining for another. It turned out to be not about the loss of a lover, but about the loss of the Tibetan language. Its purpose was to remind people that the Tibetan language was precious and that all should continue learning it.

We met halfway in our traditions, non-Tibetans trying a different way of celebrating, Tibetan Americans making an effort to educate, share, and include us. As we put on our coats and thanked our hosts, we guests felt fortunate, conscious of how few other people in the cold, dark city were celebrating in the manner of people miles and millennia away. I stepped outside. The few leaves clinging to the bare oak tree whispered and spirits stirred. Each leaf held a glint of moonlight, a gift for me to see, if I would simply look up.

CHAPTER 11

◝

A Curriculum for Saving Tibet

A people without the knowledge of their past history, origin
and culture is like a tree without roots.
—MARCUS GARVEY, EARLY-TWENTIETH-CENTURY
AFRICAN AMERICAN LEADER AND ACTIVIST

Tibetan American New Year celebrations were centered around ancient and living Tibetan customs, sprinkled with just a few new traditions from the United States. But Tibetan American birthday parties seemed just the opposite—modeled after American customs, with a few sprinkles of Tibetan culture. Birthdays for children were not celebrated in old Tibet nor in early exile settlements of India and Nepal. Many older immigrants didn't even know the dates of their birth, perhaps born at home to parents who didn't record that information in writing or who were schooled by their religion to believe in the insignificance of the individual. Migmar knew he was born on a Tuesday, because *Migmar* means "Tuesday" in Tibetan. When he was required to put his date of birth on a form, he estimated as best he could. When Tenzin filled out her husband's US visa application, however, she couldn't remember what date he had been using, so she created yet another birth date for him. He invariably laughed when someone asked for his birth date, as if he knew they didn't have time for the full explanation.

In this destination country, the Tibetan Americans I met seemed to find birthday traditions delightful, and they quickly adopted and enhanced them, combining their love of children and community celebration with the pleasures of accessible materialism. Especially one-year-olds, but also other small children, seem to merit elaborate birthday parties. In the first of these I attended, I was one of more than one hundred guests, alongside whole families, from elders to tiniest grandchildren, who crowded into the picnic shelter of a Madison park on a summer Sunday. Adults chatted near a pile of brightly packaged gifts, and dozens of children of every age, many in frilly dresses or snazzy sports shirts, played and shrieked on swing sets and teeter-totters.

"It's time for the piñata!" an older teen called. Children made a big circle around a tissue-confetti-covered donkey. I noted it was children, not adults, who directed this part of the party.

The older boys wildly whacked the donkey with the stick, as I jumped up, crying, "Stand back! Stand back!" I lined the children up, youngest first, and tried to assert some teacherly order over the crowd. "Little kids first. You, then you. Who's next oldest?" I asked. "Only three tries. Well, okay, she can have another try."

Why was I, the bossy sister, taking over? Though it would have been a chance to witness traditions in transition, I was unable to sit on the sidelines. I identified more as an aunt, responsible for seeing that the children didn't get hurt and that everyone got a turn, than as a cultural anthropologist. Time after time at Tibetan American gatherings with children present, when Tibetan and American traditions jumbled together, I would jump into the fray to make it somehow more "correct."

I held my tongue, though, when children left the piñata, its smashed innards strewn on the ground, their little hands full of candies. Since their own parents were present, I refrained from instructing them not to throw the wrappers on the ground or stuff all the sweets into their mouths at once. I left my American auntie role and resumed my American middle-class "don't discipline other people's kids in public" tight-lipped discomfort.

Finished with the piñata, kids crowded around a store-bought sheet cake, elaborately topped with sugar-coated Disney figurines. The adults beamed, seeming to enjoy the pleasures of indulging their children in something they had never had, happy to be together with many friends.

⮀

If Tibetan children in Madison were now going to birthday parties and smacking piñatas, I wondered, who was teaching them their own Tibetan customs?

In 1999, as families from India and Nepal reunited in Madison with the original "qualified, displaced Tibetans," the Wisconsin Tibetan Association launched a Saturday school to teach this new generation of children their parents' language and culture. They followed a venerated tradition of American immigrants from centuries ago to the present, with small schools in church basements or borrowed community rooms, as not only Tibetan but also Jewish, Japanese, Korean, Chinese, and other parents tried to preserve fragile homeland languages and customs.

The opening of the school attracted sixty-three students in its first year. But Tenzin's four children flatly refused to go.

"We already know all that stuff," Lhadon said, tossing her long hair behind her shoulders.

"There are better schools in India," Tamdin told me.

They continued with excuses about why they didn't want to

go, even though I knew, especially in Lhadon's case, that some of their friends had enrolled. Migmar and Tenzin wanted them to attend but shrugged their shoulders when all four presented a united, negative front.

I tried to reason with the teens about the importance of cultural preservation. "These are such precious years," I told them. "You can't go back and regain them. It's easy now for you to learn to read and write Tibetan. It will be harder later."

They could barely write the comely, curling Tibetan alphabet and certainly could not read Tibetan at any level of proficiency. Their father, with only five years of formal schooling, was able to write the cursive script confidently and read the prayers printed in tiny font in well-worn books, long out of print. By turning their noses up at the idea of extra schooling, the children were bypassing the opportunity to learn the printed (*u-chen*) script and elegantly flowing cursive forms (*gyul yig*). In its living, spoken, and written forms, the Tibetan language is close to Sanskrit, one of the most vital, ancient keys to world languages, as well as an embodiment of religion and philosophy, poetry, medicine, folk tales, songs, and chants.

"Who's going to teach your own children these traditions?" I pleaded.

"Somebody else," answered Namgyal sullenly. The teens hunched over their computer games, the English font and images gliding, flying, and flashing across the small screens.

"Why do you care?" a friend asked me, as I lamented their disinterest. "They're right. They need to get on with the business of being American."

I cared. I cared a lot. My previous work at Folklore Village, my years of travel abroad, and my professional job with world languages and international education all lasered into a passion. For me, languages and folk traditions and curiosity about other cultures unraveled secrets of how the world functioned, why people valued such contrasting things, and why people acted "differently" from one another. Further cajoling got me nowhere, however.

Despite the nonattendance of the four kids whose futures I cared about most, the Wisconsin Tibetan Association's Saturday School of Tibetan Language and Culture succeeded and prospered. I visited it in 2015, fifteen years after its inception, and met fifty-three eager-eyed children, ages six to seventeen, divided into four classrooms. I observed as they actively recited the Tibetan alphabet and took quizzes, their dark heads bent over their scripted books. In the hallways between classes they chattered with friends—in English.

"Students born here speak English like any other native-born American kid," a teacher told me.

At Tibetan American gatherings I had attended, most children spoke English to one another and to their parents; most adults, on the other hand, spoke Tibetan to one another. Some parents replied to their children in Tibetan, but most used English. In barely a single decade, children like the ones in my family, who had struggled to learn English but spoke Tibetan fluently, had given way to younger children born in the United States who spoke English fluently, but had little or only passive knowledge of Tibetan. Most of the small children were able to understand some Tibetan, but they chose to reply to their parents, grandparents, and friends in English. I was shocked to realize that the spoken Tibetan language among young people in Madison had almost disappeared, right before my eyes. By 2015, the four young people in my family had become adults, some with children of their own. Years earlier, I had fretted about their refusal to attend Saturday school, but now they were among the families who consciously and consistently spoke Tibetan at home with their own children. Like sands on the

Tibetan Plateau, my perspective shifted. I was impressed and appreciative that my family had maintained their linguistic heritage after all.

I should not have been surprised at how easily a heritage language can disappear. Decades of immigrants in the United States have followed a similar pattern, eager to speak English, often ashamed of elders who speak in broken sentences with heavy accents. Unlike children, in school all day and surrounded by English on TV and on the playgrounds, parents often have little time or opportunity to study English at length and with support. Whether a child does or doesn't use her home language depends on many things: if it is essential for communication, whether peers speak it, even whether speaking it is perceived as high or low status. Would these first-generation kids say later, like I did to my own father, that they wished they had been "made to" learn the language when it was within easy reach?

Back at the Saturday school, the principal introduced me during the morning's assembly. "This woman, Madeline-lak," he said, "is a very kind person. She has been a friend to one of our families. Please welcome her today."

I had never before been introduced for qualities of my heart, rather than for my achievements. The principal hadn't mentioned my education credentials or my attempt to gather research for a book. I realized this choice of focus echoed the famous words of the Dalai Lama—"My religion is kindness"—and I was touched to be introduced so simply.

Parents of children in the school paid twenty-five dollars per month per child and took turns preparing snacks, since the study day stretched from 9:30 a.m. to 2:30 p.m. The five college-educated teachers each received a tiny honorarium. The woman who instructed dance, with an impressive two decades of professional experience, had been specifically recruited by the Wisconsin Tibetan Association all the way from the dance ensemble at the prestigious Tibetan Institute of Performing Arts in Dharamsala, India. Three dance groups, one for high school, one for middle school, and one for younger children, seemed to be the highlights of the students' school day, boys participating as enthusiastically as girls.

"*Kae-chenpo gyab!*" the dance teacher called out, urging them to sing louder.

Saturday school in Madison's Tibetan American community, like in many other communities across the United States, is divided into five academic levels. Beginning as young as age six, students spend two years at each level before finishing around age sixteen or sometime in high school. The curriculum focuses on Tibetan language, including reading, writing, and speaking. It encompasses a cursory introduction to Buddhism, where students learn basic prayers, symbols, and philosophy, as well as stories about the Buddha. One of the founding teachers, Kelsang Gyatso Kunor, has labored over a Tibetan history text, written for Tibetan kids "who are born in a faraway country and have never seen Tibet." With modern and archival photos of rivers, mountains, regional clothing styles, arts, and musical instruments, it tries to bring to life a history, beginning in 127 BCE with the first of Tibet's forty-five kings.

"Students are surprised by Tibet's former size, that it covered one-third of contemporary China," Genlak Kelsang Gyatso said. "They can't see it on today's maps, so they have the impression it was just some small, barren desert." The curriculum links students with their parents' knowledge—dialects, songs, proverbs, prayers, recipes, and riddles—and gives a context for items in family closets, hanging on walls, or atop shelves of the shrine.

"This school is something I look forward to every week," said a middle school student called Kunsel. She had been enrolled since she was six. "I have a whole different group of friends here."

"The most important thing to me is learning the language," explained Loten, a male high school student, also an enrollee since age six.

Both Loten and Kunsel admitted they knew many Tibetan Americans their age who did not attend the school.

"They imagine all the kids here know Tibetan and that they'll be the only ones who can't speak," Kunsel said. "But it's not true. We're all just learning."

Loten and Kunsel told me that many of the families whose children didn't attend Saturday school also didn't tend to come to the celebration gatherings of the Wisconsin Tibetan Association. Family by family, a small percentage of southern Wisconsin's Tibetan American community seemed to be absenting themselves from the Tibetan part of being Tibetan American. When I asked why some families didn't participate more, teachers at the school speculated that perhaps, with their multiple jobs, the parents simply didn't have time. Or, if they had multiple children, maybe the combined monthly fee seemed too high. Maybe they thought, what's the point? Was it really so important to speak Tibetan? Would it really make a difference to Tibet's future or to their children's?

That the school had survived and prospered was no small feat. Over half of Tibetan American students enrolled in area public schools attended the weekend school, an impressive statistic among cities with similar-sized Tibetan American communities. When I talked with teachers, it sounded like the challenges the school faced were identical to those of Saturday schools of many other immigrant groups, both past and present: difficulty in finding teachers, updating instructors' often old-fashioned ways of teaching language, creating materials relevant to children in the United States, locating inexpensive places to meet, and raising funds. The Tibetan American community faced another significant challenge. Unless adults could imbue their children with a love for the Tibetan language, an appreciation for Tibetan Buddhism's ancient and deep religious and philosophic traditions, and a passion for Tibet's survival, whether within China or within the Tibetan diaspora, these ideas would disappear. How could small children understand or accept responsibility for survival of Tibetan culture?

Displaced Tibetans had given much thought to education in the years since they had left Tibet. Their fourteen-page "Basic Education Policy for Tibetans in Exile," written in 1997 by Professor Samdhong Rinpoche, afterwards reviewed, debated, and passed by the India-based Tibetan Parliament in Exile, has stood up well against time. As Rinpoche wrote, "The general purpose of education is to awaken and develop the human qualities of wisdom, loving kindness and compassion; their dependent virtues of right view and conduct; and the art of creativity and innovation."

The Dalai Lama and leading Tibetan educators such as Professor Rinpoche speak eloquently of the two wings each student needs to fly. One symbolizes the rigorous, modern academic curriculum of the nations in which Tibetans live in exile, while the other holds aloft Tibetans' traditional ways of learning compassion, values, and nonviolence. The "Basic Education Policy" originally stated,

> The ultimate goal of the Tibetan people is to transform the whole of the three *Cholkhas* (provinces) of Tibet into a zone of non-violence (*ahimsa*) and peace; to transform Tibetan society into a non-violent society; and to lead other peoples onto the path of non-violence and compassion. Thus, the Tibetan people must be made capable of correctly and fully understanding the direction, path and means to this goal.

It was laudable and visionary. The purpose of education was to develop compassionate, nonviolent human beings who could, in turn, help create a more peaceful world. I admired the teachers, who committed weekend after weekend to their work with young people and sought advice from parents and monks to follow pathways of venerated learning traditions. It was a remarkable model for achieving peace, a road map that was easier to draw than to adhere to.

I had viewed peace memorials in Hiroshima, Japan, and stared at the flicker of the eternal flame in former World War II death camps such as Majdanek in Lublin, Poland. I had traveled far and pondered hard to understand how one teaches and reaches enduring levels of peace. As an international educator and world traveler, I felt suddenly startled to realize the scope and importance of this small Tibetan Saturday School of Language and Culture in my very own community.

Folk dance was, to my relief, one cultural thread the four children in my family had retained and nurtured throughout their early Madison years. With other teens in the Tibetan American community, the three older kids, Namgyal, Lhadon, and Tamdin, and later Thardoe when he entered high school, organized Madison's first Tibetan American performing group at West High School, completely on their own initiative. Tamdin helped with choreography of "So Ya La," a dance he had performed in a similar group in India. With authentic costumes borrowed from a Tibetan American dance group in Chicago, they stomped, swirled, and sang at festivals and school fairs, without instrument accompaniment, their voices clear and strong, their long sleeves flying back and forth. In the enthusiastic audience, the hearts of parents and people like me swelled to see their energy, their talent, and the flame of heritage burning brightly.

⁓

CHAPTER 12

Double Wedding

Wherever you have friends, that's your country, and wherever you receive love, that's your home.
—TIBETAN PROVERB, CITED BY DALAI LAMA XIV
IN *THE BOOK OF JOY*

In 2006 I left Madison, for what ended up being six years, to work abroad in Africa and central Asia, before ending up in the Peace Corps headquarters in Washington, DC, for a time. One of my strengths (and therefore weaknesses) is full involvement in places where I land. My contact during these years with Tenzin's family was less than one might have imagined—a phone call or two and public letters that I sent to a list of hundreds, unsure if anyone in Tenzin's family even read them. The four kids, now young adults, worked jobs at grocery stores, senior care facilities, and hospital maintenance departments while struggling on with their educations. Tamdin finished college at the University of Wisconsin–Eau Claire, majoring in art; the others tackled certification courses at the area technical college. Then in 2010, I got a phone call: the oldest and youngest brothers, Namgyal and Thardoe, would celebrate their marriages in a double wedding in Madison. Wild horses on the Tibetan

Plateau could not have kept me away. I flew home from DC to return for a glorious summer weekend.

Both brothers were marrying the young women they had met in India during my time there in 2005 as an auntly chaperone. Namgyal was marrying Lhakpa from Dharamsala, and Thardoe was marrying Samkyi, his childhood friend from the south Indian settlement.

Namgyal and Lhakpa's marriage was close to what might be called an arranged marriage, the product of recommendations from family friends and from parental telephone calls, reinforced with their actual face-to-face meeting. Thardoe's marriage, by contrast, a so-called love marriage, was inspired by infatuation with a girl he had taken a fancy to. The two ways of meeting remain common throughout Asia and diaspora communities. Regardless of how they had found their matches, both young men were giddy with love on their wedding day.

I was disappointed to realize how out of touch I had been. Both couples had already celebrated weddings in India. Namgyal and Lhakpa's was a big affair, with hundreds of Dharamsala friends and families in attendance. Thardoe and Samkyi's had been smaller, but both brides had shed many tears, as their travel to the United States on spousal visas would follow shortly. Having weddings in the women's hometowns not only enabled friends and family to personally bid them congratulations and farewell, but also facilitated the visa process, since a spousal visa has a higher chance of being approved than a fiancée visa. The weddings also ensured the propriety of living together, since both new brides initially moved into the home of Tenzin and Migmar, now with all its four bedrooms full to bulging. Lhadon was delighted to have two new sisters-in-law in the house.

Of the two brides, Lhakpa arrived first and became pregnant a year later, about the same time that her cousin and now sister-in-law Samkyi entered the United States with her finally approved visa. With the nod of Deer Park Tibetan Buddhist monks, the couples chose July 24, 2010, to celebrate their unions within the Madison community, and Tenzin and Migmar invited three hundred friends and family. The shared wedding tied together many threads of happiness—brother and brother, north India cousin and south India cousin, Tibetan Indians and Tibetan Americans, and weddings held on two continents. My family was expanding, continuing to integrate itself into the midwestern landscape while still retaining important Tibetan ties.

The double wedding was a perfect homecoming for me, after spending three years in the parched, dry mountains of Lesotho, Africa's "Mountain Kingdom," as a Peace Corps volunteer, and then accepting a job in fast-paced Washington, DC, at Peace Corps headquarters. Madison's greenery and shimmering lakes contrasted with Lesotho's meager villages and Washington's hurtling traffic. It was comforting to see how solidly and successfully Tenzin's family had built their lives, and how carefully they treasured and nurtured the ties between West and East. As soon as the wedding date was set, Tenzin and Migmar had tapped into their savings to arrange a shopping trip to India to buy things not yet available in the United States.

I was amazed that people who lived so modestly would travel abroad just to shop. "What did you need to buy that you couldn't get here?" I asked when I heard the story.

Tenzin recited the shopping list, mixing Tibetan and English. "We needed a *bo*, nice *chupa*, *shamo*, *taiyun tagyak*, and long, long *khata*." She was referring to *chemar bo*, the wooden container to hold barley and wheat to greet the guests; *shamo* (*shamo gasse*), the traditional fox fur–lined wedding hats for the brides and grooms; and *chupa*, both the lovely, pastel silk *chupa* dresses for the brides and the heavy wool, silk-lined *chupa* jackets for the grooms. There needed to be a silver wedding tea set (*taiyun tagyak*) and yards of silken cloth to cut into *khata* for the guests to give to the bridal pairs and for the bridal pairs to give back to departing guests. Tenzin and Migmar went to India and returned. Along with Migmar, who was a skilled cook, the four women in the household began planning the wedding menu and week of festivities.

In Chicago, brother Tamdin was living with his girlfriend Tseten, and Tseten's mother regularly catered for Chicago's many Tibetan American events. On the day of the wedding, ten families helped with the cooking under Tseten's mother's direction. The wedding table sagged with piles of braided white buns called *tingmo*, lamb curry, fried beef, chili chicken, a Tibetan rendering of chow mein, a spicy Indian black bean dish called *kalachana*, four hundred hand-shaped and cookie-like *kapse*, and no fewer than two thousand hand-made *momo* (meat dumplings).

"I'll elope," Lhadon joked. "This is too much work."

The wedding was held in a community center just outside Madison. As guests arrived, we were greeted by Lhakpa's sister, who had flown in from London, and a male friend of the brothers, both wearing traditional *chupas*. They held the new *chemar bo* that Tenzin and Migmar had purchased in India. They gently instructed me and a few other non-Tibetan guests on how to offer a blessing for the brides and grooms. "Touch this barley flour to your forehead. Now take a few of these barley grains and touch your forehead again." Again, as we'd done during Losar, the New Year's celebrations, we repeated the prayer for their good fortune, good health, and long life.

Inside the hall, the festive spirit was intensified by the rainbow of colors on women's *pangden*, the traditional aprons worn for special occasions. I proudly wore a *pangden* and jumper-style *chupa* as well, borrowed from the array that hung in

Tenzin's closet. Tsetan, Tamdin's girlfriend, saw me enter and came forward to serve a cup of sweet, black Tibetan tea and a bowl of sweet rice, called *dre sil*, cooked with coconut and raisins. Since Tibetan rice is usually served plain, this dish was served to bring sweetness to the lives of the marrying couples. Tsetan's mother was a blur of motion as she directed the placement of dozens of simmering roaster ovens and commanded her sons, who hefted heavy pots and staffed the bar. Samkyi's older brother Jampa Khedup, who had trained as a Buddhist monk and now worked as a Tibetan language instructor at the University of Wisconsin, acted as the day's smiling, jocular emcee. Everyone called him Genlak (teacher). Genlak Jampa called the guests to order and announced the single-file entry of the wedding procession.

"The parents of the grooms, Migmar Dorjee and Tenzin Kalsang!" Genlak Jampa proclaimed into the microphone. I had never seen Tenzin and Migmar more handsomely clad or looking more proud as when they walked past admiring guests to the front of the room.

Sadly, though, the parents of both brides were absent. Samkyi's mother was ill and her father deceased; Lhakpa's parents' visas had been denied, victim to the increasingly stringent, post-9/11 US security restrictions. Lhakpa was doubly disappointed. She had hoped her mother could not only attend the wedding in America but also stay for the birth of her first child, due in a month. Thankfully, Lhakpa's parents and Samkyi's mother had been central to the celebrations that had taken place in India.

"And now," Genlak Jampa said, "please welcome the grooms and brides!" Guests remained standing as the two couples entered, and the loud applause spilled out into the green fields that surrounded the center.

The couples each bowed in front of the Buddhist altar, with

its huge framed portrait of His Holiness the Fourteenth Dalai Lama, whose smile beamed upon the whole room. They took seats at the front of the hall on a pair of plush leather sofas. After various introductions, Genlak Jampa announced the beginning of the blessing ceremony, and guests lined up to present *khata*, first upon the altar in front of the Dalai Lama's portrait, then to each of the brides and grooms.

Migmar and Tenzin went first and bent low over each of their sons and new daughters-in-law, murmuring prayerful expressions in Tibetan. As honorary auntie, I was included among the family members who came next in line. "Bless you and good luck," I whispered to the brides, putting a *khata* around each of their necks. "I am so proud of you," I said to Namgyal and then to Thardoe, as memories of their childhood coalesced into sudden tears.

The brides and grooms were radiant and clear-eyed. The brides' tears had spilled earlier, at their weddings back in India, when Samkyi and Lhakpa had bid farewell not only to their families, but also to their childhood neighborhoods, their country of birth, the entire Asian continent. Lhakpa told me she cried for nine hours straight, sitting in the Delhi airport as their flight to the United States was delayed several times. Beside her, Namgyal sat stoic and determined.

Tears of brides have flowed over many centuries, especially in the old days in Tibet, when a bride would travel to live with her husband's family in his village and might only rarely have a chance to visit her family home. Rural weddings there might still take six days, Migmar related—three days at the bride's village, then three days at the groom's. During Migmar's childhood, the home of the bride filled with songs that honored her and her parents and made references to nature, Buddhism, and ancient Tibetan myths. They were songs these four young people and their generation of peers had never learned.

My own grandparents left their Czech-Polish border town of Cieszyn after their wedding in 1920, never to return to see their country or their families. Lhakpa and Samkyi, by contrast, could fly back to India to visit their families. They could travel to New York City, Toronto, and London, where fate had flung their sisters and brothers. Indeed, Samkyi would be on her way back to India shortly, since learning of her mother's cancer diagnosis. Nonetheless, Lhakpa's and Samkyi's choices to marry a spouse and make a home in another country gave this ceremony a feeling of solemnity that I had seldom felt at other weddings. It seemed to be a further severing of cultural ties to Tibet—from India, where Tibetans in exile numbered over 110,000, to Madison, where they formed a community of about 500. Even taking the United States as a whole, the total number of Tibetans Americans clustered in many different states is less than 10,000.

As guests returned to their seats after the blessing ceremony to enjoy the meal, the room filled with animated Tibetan dialects, as well as English, Nepali, and Hindi. Looking around to see so few other non-Tibetan faces, I marveled that this was taking place in a midwestern community. This, too, was Wisconsin.

The emcee called selected guests forward to sing in Tibetan and Hindi. A brother and a sister sang a duet called "Chang Shey" ("Wine Song"). A man named Monlam sang a Tibetan love song whose lyrics had been written in the late 1600s by the Sixth Dalai Lama, who, guests told me, loved to write poetry. A well-known singer later put his poems to music, and this particular song graces many traditional occasions. The lyrics describe a man's glance at a beautiful girl, Rinzin Wangmo, only to find her glancing at him at the same time. Romantic lyrics from centuries long past softened the boisterous joviality in the room.

"Here in the US," one guest told me over the applause, "there are more and more Hindi and Tibetan pop songs at weddings, and fewer of these old songs."

Amidst more hand-clapping, the couples cut and fed one another pieces of two identical wedding cakes. Just as I was feeling secure in the familiarity of American wedding customs, hands reached out to pull me and the other guests into a huge circle of folk dancing. I did my best to imitate the graceful steps and stomps of older men and women who jostled me along as the singing circles moved right, then left, then right again. Dancers waved their arms over their heads and did full turns, as I tried to catch on, usually a half beat late.

Several younger women brushed past me as the dance circle dissolved after an hour of merry movement. They had changed from their *chupa* into sequined miniskirts and cocktail dresses. The grooms and other young men had re-emerged in suits and ties. Lights dimmed, strobe lights flickered, and the younger generation thronged to the floor to shake and shout to a DJ's full-volume disco music in English and Hindi. Older folks retired to the tables to chat and comment on the gyrations, no doubt forming opinions about future matches of their children and grandchildren. In the shadows, a few friends of the couples carried armfuls of *khata* to a waiting table by the door. Long past midnight, as the guests finally left, the wedding couples draped *khata* around the necks of each departing person and thanked him or her for coming and for being part of their new lives in America. I wondered if Tibetans had a saying like my grandparents' people had: "To have danced at a Polish wedding is to be friends forever."

I walked outside, where moonlight flooded the fields and parking lot. The summer night was lush, a new baby coming soon. My friendship with this family felt full, round, and verdant.

⟶

Migmar and Tenzin felt enormous pride in seeing their sons wedded to young women from ethnic Tibetan families of good standing. I had seen how Tenzin's family and telephone networks had connected Namgyal to Lhakpa. When Tenzin found out, however, that youngest son Thardoe had ventured back to his childhood neighborhood in southern India on his own to search out the pretty girl he remembered, she had grabbed her cell phone to contact neighbors and relatives. Alarmed, she tried to find out everything she could about Samkyi's family, their finances, and their reputation. Equally alarmed, Samkyi's mother back in India did the same.

Samkyi had a degree in computer applications from Bangalore University in India. In Madison, she immediately landed a couple of internships, then a computer job with the University of Wisconsin–Extension. She was soon serving as an officer in the Wisconsin Tibetan Association and was elected general secretary for one of the eleven regional chapters of the newly formed Tibetan Youth Congress, an international nongovernmental organization with eighty-seven branches in ten countries. Samkyi has a gentle, gifted way of organizing and advising. She is a living example of Gandhi's words, "Be the change you want to see in the world."

Samkyi's dedication to Buddhist practice inspired Thardoe to join her commitment to vegetarianism. On the next Thanksgiving at my house, Samkyi arrived with a vegetable entree and a turkey-shaped tofu dish. I felt guilty about the savory poultry aromas suffusing the house. Thardoe, who had been an enthusiastic turkey eater at past Thanksgivings, passed by the overflowing platter with barely a glance and filled his plate with salads, vegetables, and the "tofurkey."

Lhakpa had a degree in accounting from the University of

Delhi, but it was the education commitments of her parents that awed me. Her father and mother had fled Tibet in 1959 at ages eight and ten, respectively. Her mother had never, in all her life, had an opportunity to go to school. With the death of his own parents at an early age, her father had been taken in by a monk in the border country of Bhutan and schooled to a level that, by the time he came to Dharamsala in his early thirties, qualified him for a job as departmental editor of oral history in the Library of Tibetan Works and Archives. He dedicated his efforts to building the reputation and holdings of this well-respected institution, and his daughter Tsamchoe, whom Susan and I had met in India, also worked there for a time. Lhakpa's mother had become a successful businesswoman, running a shop in Delhi that sold handbags in the summer and jackets in the winter. All seven of their children were college-educated. I saw the strength of Lhakpa's commitment to schooling when she enrolled at Madison's technical college soon after her arrival. Despite longing for her parents and family back in India, despite working every possible hour in a senior care center, navigating a new culture, and buying a house, and through two pregnancies and the births of her daughter and son, Lhakpa studied long into the nights and weekends to earn two degrees in nursing. She is an imperturbable earth mother, with a low voice and a laugh that gurgles like a mountain brook. She is quick to admire and encourage others. Namgyal had been her first and only boyfriend.

Moving to the United States, Lhakpa told me, had been often difficult and strange. "I felt like a foreigner in the grocery store and in the malls," she said. "Suddenly I saw I was a minority. I couldn't get used to the disrespect of students at school. They listened to lectures with their feet up on the desks in front of them. They called teachers by their first names. When Choesang was first born, and everyone else in the house was working, I was home all alone every single night. I cried like crazy."

She looked around her new home. A pot of tea for me warmed on the stove; children's drawings were scotch-taped floor to ceiling on a kitchen wall.

"Between Namgyal and me, we have a good rhythm," Lhakpa said. "We're a good match. We will make it work."

CHAPTER 13

~

Search for the Middle Way

*It is not required of you to complete the work, but neither
are you free to desist from it.*
—RABBI TARPHON, AS QUOTED IN *PIRKEI AVOT*
(*ETHICS OF THE FATHERS*)

In Chicago, fifty Tibetan Americans got off a bus, bundling
their nylon coats and leather jackets against the icy winds off
Lake Michigan. Among them, Thardoe and his wife, Samkyi,
shouldered their daypacks and pulled placards from storage
under the bus: Free Tibet! China Out of Tibet! Stop Murder of
Monks and Nuns!

Hoisting the signs over their shoulders, the protesters
headed for the Consulate of the People's Republic of China with
firm steps, grateful for the companionship and commitment of
those who had chosen to come. They had taken leave from work
to be in Chicago on a weekday so they would be visible to Chinese staff working inside the consulate. Their goal was to show
that Tibetans in America had not given up on freeing their
ancestral country. The activists included non-Tibetans as well:
Students for a Free Tibet, university instructors, and male and
female practitioners of Buddhism, some in burgundy robes with
heads shaved.

Outside the consulate, the protesters formed a circle on the sidewalk and began shouting slogans, holding their placards high. They attempted to hand flyers explaining the history of this day, March 10, Tibetan Uprising Day, to mostly disinterested passersby. "On March 10, 1959, tens of thousands of Tibetans took to the streets of Lhasa, Tibet's capital, rising up against China's illegal invasion and occupation of their homeland," explained the flyer. "They surrounded the Potala Palace, the home of the Dalai Lama, to protect his life and the future of the Tibetan nation." In the decades since, March 10 has become an annual day of protest. Tibetans in exile and their allies gather in capital cities in North America, Europe, Asia, and Australia and in Tibetan settlements across India, Bhutan, and Nepal to speak passionately for the freedom of a nation whose independence seems a receding dream. At greater risk for doing so, Tibetans within Tibet dare to demonstrate on this day as well, and the government of China shuts down access to the Tibet Autonomous Region to foreign tourists for the month of March, due to the potential for unrest and police reactions to it.

While Thardoe and Samkyi were with the group in Chicago, Migmar and Tenzin were marching 150 miles away, in Madison, in front of the City County Building. There, by proclamation of the mayor and the state legislature, the day had been declared Tibetan Uprising Day, and a Tibetan flag joined the bright blue state flag to fly over the city. These symbolic gestures, barely noticeable in a city whose calendar is peppered with demonstrations and commemorations, are important to the Tibetan American community. Each year, I noted the contrast between the joy of the Tibetan New Year, usually in February, and the more somber, strident tones of Tibetan Uprising Day the following month.

While the goals of the two groups of protesters were similar, their approaches showcased vigorous debate within the Tibetan diaspora communities and a generational divide. The activists in Chicago were making a direct demand for Tibet's full independence, or *rangzen* in Tibetan; the Madison group supported a proposed political compromise called the Middle Way. The Middle Way is a proposal to relinquish complete independence for Tibet as a nation, instead advocating for the creation of a harmonious National Autonomous Zone for Tibet within China's borders. The Dalai Lama and ministers of the Tibetan Administration outlined this compromise in the Five Point Peace Plan of 1987, following decades of debate and negotiation. The plan would make Tibet an international zone of peace and nonviolence, but so far the Chinese government has not responded.

"Older people follow the Dalai Lama's Middle Way," Samkyi explained to me in her gentle voice. She was active as a local and regional officer of the Tibetan Youth Congress. "Even though Thardoe supports my activism, demanding full independence for Tibet, I know in his heart he believes instead in the Middle Way.

"Young people want to be activist, but at the same time we are, like the Dalai Lama, committed to nonviolence." She sighed. "I feel pulled both ways."

Samkyi outlined the proposal to me point by point, something many Tibetans in exile can do. One prong calls for the immediate stop of the Chinese government's practice of transferring ethnic Han Chinese into Tibet, rendering ethnic Tibetans a minority in their own homeland. The second point proposes human rights and democratic freedoms, to ensure that Tibetan history, language, and culture can be taught in schools and that practicing them will no longer be grounds for imprisonment. The plan also calls for the protection and restoration of Tibet's once-pristine landscapes and calls for abandonment of China's use of the Tibetan region for dumping of nuclear waste and manufacturing of nuclear weapons. In return, the proposal acknowledges China's military, political, and international sovereignty over Tibet.

Like Thardoe and his parents, I too leaned toward the Middle Way, a great vision, yet nonetheless a painful compromise for Tibetans in exile. Many others had grown tired of the lack of progress for the plan. As activists have asked older leaders, what have six decades of peaceful nonviolence accomplished?

Not wanting to detract from one another's messages, though, the two groups of Tibetan Americans head in different directions on March 10. Few Americans might realize the disparity in their appeals, perhaps wondering, if they wondered at all, how so few could stand up to the might of a government of so many. But both groups hoped someone was listening, in particular that imagined powerhouse, the international community, which included me.

I did not feel powerful on this issue. I felt, as an Arabic proverb muttered, like a grain of sand beneath the camel's hoof. Still, mighty sandstorms can blow from tiny grains of sand. Samkyi and Thardoe's persistence, patience, and courage made me want to stand taller and speak up louder.

⁓

In their work for progress, the Tibetan Youth Congress (TYC) has documented that Tibetans in Tibet languish by the thousands in prison barracks. Increasingly, young people in Tibet, who must study Chinese language and history at school, are no longer fully fluent in their own language. Han Chinese and other ethnicities continue to settle within Tibetan regions by the thousands, and the government promotes marriages between Tibetans and Han Chinese. TYC members, among scholars and human rights activists, accuse China of cultural genocide.

"Things are really desperate," Samkyi insists.

Yet, just as with any husband and wife who disagree on politics, she and Thardoe try to keep their disagreements pointed but civil. "When our discussions about it get heated, we say 'Let's stop,'" says Thardoe, ever conciliatory.

"Sometimes those discussions help," admits Samkyi, who like her husband is also a natural mediator. "I have to defend what I think. It would be boring if both of us thought the same way."

I was able to feel some of the younger couple's sense of urgency and despair during the summers of 2011 to 2014 when more than 130 Tibetans, mostly in Tibet but also in Nepal and Bhutan, doused themselves with gasoline and set themselves aflame in protest. Whether in front of temples, in outdoor markets, or on the grounds of government buildings, horrified on-lookers screamed. Some threw themselves upon the burning person. The first immolations were barely covered by the international press, and few of my non-Tibet-interested friends had heard about them. Some who burned themselves were nuns and monks in their forties and fifties, but many were younger monks and men in their twenties, an age of passion and activism. These Tibetans, some from nomadic families, expressed the hopelessness of their political situation by committing a desperate individual act. The Chinese government denounced the political suicides, made immolation a criminal act, and named the perpetrators as terrorists. Officials condemned families and communities from which they came and accused the Security Office in Dharamsala of helping would-be immolators plan and maximize publicity.

In China, female activist Tsering Woeser chronicled every suicide in her blog, until it was taken down by the Chinese government. By then, ordinary citizens within China had caught wind of the postings and added their alarm. On YouTube and other websites, I found faces, names, and ages of those who chose this terrible death. Addressing how people who believe in nonviolence could end their lives this way, Woeser wrote in her book *Tibet on Fire: Self-Immolations Against Chinese Rule*, "These protestors undergo the ultimate pain of burning each and every cell of their bodies, without harming other living beings, simply to make their voices and grievances heard."

~

Long before the years of self-immolations, I asked Thardoe and his brothers and sister, "What does it feel like to know that people expect you to play some role in the struggle to free Tibet?" As children, they would frown and shrug, but over the years, they approached this occasional question of mine more thoughtfully.

In one conversation, Thardoe told me he recalled seeing the protests of Tibetans in Tibet on television in India when he was still in elementary school. "I saw monks running, police chasing them and beating them for nothing. Those video clips touched my heart. How can some people torture others?

"I don't feel guilty about Tibet today, I feel sad," he continued. "Here in America, we don't have much burden. People living in Tibet, they have to survive against more challenges. Tibetans are less equal as citizens in their own country than the Chinese.

"But I do feel angry when people don't show up for a protest or event that we organize here in America. Tibetans in Tibet are protesting, being put behind bars. But Tibetan people living here don't want to give up even one day, even a few hours, to stand in solidarity. Adults who stand up would encourage younger people to be more active."

Perhaps Samkyi's upbringing accounted for her willingness to step forward. Her father in India was a local community leader, so she grew up understanding how local debates and grassroots organizing in time become larger movements. Her education, not only about Tibet's history but also its written and spoken language, prayers, customs, and holiday traditions, went deep. The first time she sang "Rigshengi Metok" at a local New Year's celebration, everyone, even her own family members, was startled not only that they had such a gifted singer among them, but also that she had chosen a song with a strong message for retaining Tibetan culture.

Samkyi estimated that about half of Tibetan Americans younger than fifty are members of the Tibetan Youth Congress. "Tibetans are a close-knit people, like a family. When I moved to the US, I felt—most of us feel—that we have a responsibility to Tibet and Tibetans to do something, whether to keep the Tibetan language and culture alive or to keep the Tibetan struggle alive. But if I were to accept the Middle Way, and be just a citizen of China, it would be too painful, at least for me—to stand under the Chinese flag, to sing its anthem in a country that has killed so many of my brothers and sisters."

‿

When the children were teens, Namgyal often told me matter-of-factly, "I hate all Chinese people" or "I want to kill Chinese people." The sentiment echoed the overdramatic tone often used by kids that age, and while I didn't believe he meant it literally, I knew the anger was real.

When the teens had first come to Madison in 1999, all four were in my car on an overcast day as I drove through the university campus. I slowed to a stop when I saw a lone man walking by the side of the road, already soaked in the torrent of sudden rain. Thardoe, who had been in the front seat, opened his door and crammed in with his siblings in the back, as the dripping passenger gratefully accepted the ride.

"Where are you from?" I asked the man. He took off his glasses to wipe them dry. "China," he answered.

I heard audible gasps from the backseat. Here, in the car, was the enemy.

I pointed to the backseat. "The kids are all Tibetan. They are opposed to China's policy's against Tibet."

He nodded. He turned his body so he could see all of them. "I, too, am very opposed to my country's policies against Tibet," he said in a quiet voice. "I admire Tibet very much. Someday I would love to visit there. I have only seen pictures. It is very beautiful."

There was silence in the back. The man, a graduate student at the University of Wisconsin, wasn't going far. I let him out soon after, glad that the first Chinese person they had met in America was maybe not such an enemy after all.

Conversely, even I had trouble maintaining an attitude of equanimity after we met Ani Pachen at a book signing for her newly published memoir, *Sorrow Mountain: The Journey of a Tibetan Warrior Nun*. *Ani* in Tibetan is the honorific address for a nun or other respected older woman. In her midsixties, Ani Pachen talked in a gentle, low voice, and her shining eyes radiated peace. Held for twenty-one years in Chinese prisons for her political activism, she told stories that made me want to vomit—being swung back and forth while blindfolded, beaten as she hung from a rope by her feet. Namgyal and Thardoe and I bit our lips as we listened. It was difficult to take to heart Ani Pachen's words of spiritual compassion and forgiveness for her tormentors.

I began to hear first- and secondhand accounts of abuse of Tibetans in Tibet from their friends and relatives who had come to Madison. The victims had names; the anecdotes of abuse had dates and locations. Therefore, when I myself accepted a work invitation in 2005 to attend an education conference in the

People's Republic of China, I felt guilty. Even though I would be gone for more than a month, I didn't mention to Tenzin's family where I was headed.

~

Our plane landed in a soupy yellow smog in Beijing, so thick that I vowed immediately I would never work in this city, no matter how high a salary I might be offered. But first impressions are inevitably shallow. Like too many Americans, my images of China were outdated by decades. I was awed by the fabulous skyscrapers, by the fashionable women in modern shopping malls, by the focused, exuberant, urban pace, and by the ambitious construction projects in all directions. The conference was exciting, full of new ideas about teaching world languages and educating children. Our conference hosts were kind, concerned for our comfort, and better informed than I on international education issues. Following the meetings, we were invited to enjoy "the world's largest city, Shanghai," to marvel at the phenomenal excavation of terracotta warriors in Xi'an, and to stroll on the Great Wall of China.

In our pre-China orientation, our education group had been cautioned to be sensitive to our hosts' politics. "Do not mention the three T's—Tibet, Taiwan, or Tiananmen Square." By and large I complied. Riding a public bus or waiting at train stations away from the conference, though, I struck up conversations with young people sitting next to me. They were invariably polite and impressed me with their smooth English. But if I raised the topic of Tibet, they sighed and shook their heads.

"You foreigners have all been brainwashed," they told me. "These atrocities never happened. Before Mao, Tibet was a poor, backward, feudal country. Peasants worked practically as slaves. Tibet has always been part of China. Today it is being brought into a position to share our progress. It is not true that it has jails filled with dissidents. You are getting your facts from biased sources, from the Dalai gang."

I let the comments pass or attempted to refute them with anecdotes of the family back home. The young Chinese dismissed me with impatient sighs and physically turned away, leaving me suspended in the wide, deep gulf between contemporary Chinese and its exiles.

Overwhelmed by the vast cities, I yearned to see some of rural China before I left. Naturally, I wanted to tour Tibet Autonomous Region, also called Xizang Autonomous Region, but the timing was wrong. I would wait to see that special place together with Migmar and Tenzin, if ever they could obtain travel visas.

Leaving Beijing, I joined a small group of Europeans who were headed for trekking through mountainous villages in southwestern China. An energetic, enterprising Australian guide named Nari led us, adding to her rudimentary Chinese as she went. She hired local teachers at each site who, always in excellent English, fascinated us with the tumultuous history of Yunnan Province, home to twenty-four of China's recognized fifty-seven minorities.

I was surprised to hear the Tibetan language being spoken in many towns and to see women wearing *chupas* as they worked in fields or stood in ragged lines to pass buckets of gravel to build roads. I had stepped into a part of China with centuries of connections to Tibet. Parts of Yunnan Province, as well as neighboring Sichuan Province, had been included in Kahm, one of the three major regions of former Tibet. Like the Tibetans, many of the Yi, Bai, Shaanxi, Dongba, and Naxi people in Yunnan spoke Chinese as a second language, if they spoke it at all.

Picturesque villages tumbled off mountainsides, amidst corn, potato, and tobacco fields. It was a botanist's dream, with three thousand plant species and four hundred types of trees.

Mountain azaleas, rhododendrons, quinces, mulberry bushes, plums, and orchids seemed to have timed their blossoms just for our passing. *National Geographic Magazine* had called this area one of the world's "hotspots," meaning a region on earth having the richest and most threatened reservoirs of plant and animal life. Our van stopped at Zhongdian, its Chinese name (since renamed Shangri-la to increase tourism), but called Gyelthang by the three hundred thousand people, mostly of Tibetan ethnicity who lived there. It had once been a major settlement on the trade route that linked Lhasa to eastern Tibet and countries as far away as Pakistan.

"Don't walk in the Tibetan settlement nearest the monastery," said Nari, sensitive to her role to keep tourists and ethnic Tibetans separate, "but otherwise, enjoy Songzhalin Monastery, the largest Tibetan-Buddhist monastery in Yunnan Province. It was renovated in the early 1980s, having been battered by the Red Army during the Cultural Revolution. Seven hundred monks call it their home, though only two hundred might be in residence at any time. China's 'one child policy' ended the practice of large families designating one child to become a monk."

The monastery sat magnificently atop a hill, and its exterior was painted in golden yellows and burnt oranges. The interior was dark, and as if walking in a mysterious maze, I passed Buddha statues, butter lamps, silver incense burners, and hanging *thangka*. A group of friendly young monks celebrating a lama's promotion invited us to join them for lunch.

That night, tired from hiking up stairs, cobbled walkways, and rocky paths, I went to bed early in my room in Zhongdian's Tibet Hotel. The next morning, my two Irish travel companions, James and Pip, told me they had stayed out late and strolled through Zhongdian Old Town. They had chanced upon five concentric circles of Tibetans dancing outdoors. Onlookers explained to them that city fathers had decided to revive old dances to teach them to young people. James and Pip were pulled into the circles. How I wished I hadn't been sleeping. I could picture the music, the joy, the hands held tight.

Our group headed for Tiger Leaping Gorge (Hǔ Tiào Xiá), one of the world's deepest and most spectacular river canyons, carved from a primary tributary of the Yantze River. As we hiked in pouring rain, high above the terraced fields and into the dense forests, I tried not to slip on wet stones. Droplets hurtled off the large, lobed leaves of tulip trees. Hour after hour, we hopped over widening streams and nervously checked our ankles to remove leeches. A hut appeared out of the thick forest and the local guide stopped us, pointing to the eaves from which were cascading rivulets of chilly water. "Wait here."

He came back after a few minutes.

"We'll eat lunch inside."

Relieved, we bent low to enter the modest hut, the dim light inside coming only from the open door and a single window. Two small children watched with fascination as our guide took from his backpack the unremarkable food we six tourists ate at every lunch: two loaves of bread, jars of peanut butter and jelly, a bag of fresh carrots, and bottled water. The woman of the house, dressed in black pants and a long black tunic, took from open shelves an undulating stack of tin plates that looked hand-pounded. We squatted near the small fire, though we didn't take off our still-dripping jackets. I looked around the hut, with its packed dirt floor, and itemized its sparse furnishings: a table to cook on, four stumps to sit on, and this fire ring in the center with a hole in the roof to let out smoke. In one corner on the floor was a big pile of gray blankets on a single large mattress. James spread peanut butter on a piece of bread and broke it into two pieces for the children. Their eyes widened as they ate it.

We exchanged names. The family was of the Yi ethnic group. Half of the country's eight million Yi farmed and raised animals in these ferociously steep mountains. Neighbors for centuries to Tibetan territory, their six languages were of Tibeto-Burman origins. I felt I had stepped into one of Migmar's stories of his family's subsistence on the Tibetan Plains.

The local guide translated our questions, and it was the man who answered, whether we addressed him or his wife.

"This place isn't developed," he told us.

"What are your priorities if you could make changes?" one of us asked.

"A road, electricity, a school," he replied without hesitation.

Not yet a Peace Corps volunteer, I was to encounter many elders and chiefs in remote sites who gave the same quick answer. It was a good formula for investment. Even as fast as development was pushing its way into China's rural areas, it would be a while before these three improvements made their way up this steep, isolated gorge.

As the wife passed to bring us yet another pot of tea, the guide reached up from his tree-stump seat and handed the woman a few yuan bills. Without examining them, she slipped the cash into the bodice of her tunic and bowed to him. We, who had emerged from the forested fog, were her day's unexpected gift. She was ours. Suddenly the blankets in the corner moved. A very old, thin man sat up, rubbing his eyes. The woman hurried to bring him hot tea.

～

I left China with admiration for people I had met, and with determination to study more of the country's voluminous history and magnificent literature. We trekkers separated in Lijiang, a charming UNESCO World Heritage Site, already a backpacker haven, gateway to spectacular hikes and mountain camping. Tourist shops flourished, and on the future sites of multistory hotels and major highways and railways, jackhammers sent choking dust into the air. China's fast and furious progress and the curiosity of tourists like me were erasing the very landscapes and intricate customs we had come to admire. Not just Tibetans, but other minorities in Yunnan deserved greater prosperity, better health care, electricity, and education, but in return seemed destined to give up the lands and cultural practices that defined them—their languages, poetry, proverbs, intricate dances and music, crafts, children's blessing ceremonies, burial rites, and religious practices.

Where was the Middle Way? I wondered. Where was the balance between respect for environment and the need for hospitals, roads, and electricity; between access to modern education and the right of China's many minorities to learn and practice their own vibrant traditions and languages? A Navajo person in Arizona might ask the same question, as could a southerner born in Appalachia's coal country or Louisiana's Bayou. Amnesty International has documented human rights abuses in prisons in Tibet, but the group has also documented human rights abuses in prisons in the United States, and in US-run military prisons outside the United States. I remembered the small circles of Tibetan Americans holding placards in Chicago and Madison. Citizens brave enough to protest, activists who are a thorn in the sides of governments, even ordinary persons desperate enough to set themselves aflame, remind the rest of us that humane progress demands vigilance and dissent.

On the returning flights from Beijing, I pondered cultural preservation and human rights abuse, questioning my own courage and commitment. I arrived in Madison and just missed seeing teenaged brothers Namgyal, Tamdin, and Thardoe suit up for the annual Midwest Pawo Thupten Ngodup Soccer Championship. As the brothers excitedly described their soccer victory, I once again, not in a faraway country but in my own hometown, found answers to my questions. The Middle Way, in practice, was alive and well. From the outside, their Fourth of July soccer tournament might look like just another summer sports gathering. Young and middle-aged men in colorful jerseys played on teams from cities that had become home to America's Tibetan American communities: Chicago, Minneapolis, Madison. For the young men in my family, traveling by car each summer to the rotating tournament venues gave them their first sense of North America's vastness and its great cities— first Minneapolis and Chicago, then farther to Nashville, New York, and Toronto.

On the road, the team didn't overnight in motels, but settled in with fellow Tibetan Americans who opened their homes and kitchens to the out-of-town guests. Young men met Tibetan American girls their age, compared Saturday schools, high schools, and future plans. Within the United States, they were surrounded by hundreds of adults who spoke their language and shared their nascent political convictions. Evening events at the tournaments featured long tables laden with Indian, Nepali, and Tibetan cuisine, cooked by the hosts. A concert featuring the local dance groups and favorite singers packed a hall with an audience that paid good money for tickets, attendees aware that profits would build local Tibetan American communities. Purchased off the tables near the stage, hundreds of "Free Tibet" T-shirts, caps, keychains, and bumper stickers would appear afterward to keep reminding me and other Americans of Tibet's cause.

Pawo Thupten Ngodup Championships, which include boys' basketball and girls' sports as well, are held, not only in the United States but in many countries that host Tibetan diaspora communities. The event is named for an ordinary Tibetan who became renowned after his spectacular death. He was born in 1938 in Tsang Province of Tibet and joined the famous Tashi

Lhunpo Monastery there as a boy. After fleeing Tibet in 1959, he settled in the Lugsung Samdupling Tibetan Settlement in Bylakuppe, in south India, and for twenty years, beginning in 1963, served with the Indo-Tibetan Army, before settling in a modest hut in northern Dharamsala, India. People later tried to fathom the decision that led this quiet man, who enjoyed an occasional bottle of whiskey or bout of gambling, to set himself on fire in Delhi, India, in 1998.

In the months leading up to his death, he had appeared very serious about his decision to follow the Tibetan Youth Congress delegation to Delhi to participate in a hunger strike march. The fast was getting attention from the international press, and he was assigned to the second group of fasters, to fill in the ranks when the first ones either died or, as actually happened, were disrupted by police. When police staged a second surprise raid on April 27, 1998, to break up the last three fasters, he slipped past them into an outdoor toilet, doused himself with gasoline that he had apparently stored there, lit himself on fire, and ran out into a shocked crowd, yelling slogans for Tibet's independence. As he put his hands together in a supplication of prayer, he was jumped upon by both police and fellow Tibetan exiles, all trying to put out the flames. Filmed and posted on the Internet, with a biography eloquently written by US Tibetan author and activist Jamyang Norbu, it was a death that riveted Tibetans in exile and millions far beyond India. It provided a visual of the little-publicized horrors of the Tibetan protests of that year and put into context the actions of this man who had seemed so humble and unassuming. One ordinary man showed millions that Free Tibet remained a passionate cause.

Throughout diaspora communities, anniversaries of Pawo Thupten Ngodup's death are variously marked with prayer vigils, memorial marches, speeches, and reflective writing. I liked the US-Tibetan commemoration, with hundreds of young Tibetan

Americans driving across their new homeland to play soccer and basketball, meet one another, dance, and sing. The event connected generations under an umbrella of a friendly, festive sports day, while honoring the cause of their homeland. It was a testament to hope and unity born out of bravery and despair. It was an example of how one could simultaneously move forward in a new, modern culture, while teaching and honoring the past.

As I arrived home from my trip to the People's Republic of China, greeted by photos and tales of the Madison Yak Boys' glory hours, I felt uncomfortably close to the swirling, often contradictory forces of hope, protest, and progress.

"Yeah, Madeline, you should have seen it!"

"Thardoe scored a field goal!"

As Tamdin and Namgyal enthusiastically pounded their brother on his back, my attention snapped from my musings and I joined in their cheers.

"You go, Yak Boys!"

CHAPTER 14

~

Lost Temples and Found Suitcases

The moon is brighter since the barn burned.
——Matsuo Basho, seventeenth-century
Japanese poet

As adults in the early 2000s, the three young men seemed to be living according to their own middle path—one that balanced their embrace of their new home with a groundedness in traditions from India and Tibet—through their choice of partners. In this first generation in Madison, many Tibetan Americans married other Tibetan Americans, Tibetan Indians, or Tibetan Bhutanese. Since Tibetan diaspora culture itself was fragile, uprooted, and threatened, it seemed unsurprising, even smart, for Tibetan refugees to join forces with someone who understood, for example, the importance of attending Buddhist services, or sending their children to Tibetan Saturday school, or designating an entire room for the family shrine instead of a dining room.

At the time of Thardoe's and Namgyal's double wedding, second son Tamdin and his girlfriend Tseten lived with Tseten's mother and brothers in a Chicago apartment. Tseten worked as a nurse, while Tamdin studied for his physical therapist degree. "No one commented when I moved in with her family," Tamdin told me. "They don't call me *dga rogs* [boyfriend], they call me *khyo ga* [husband]. They treat me like *khyo ga*, and I act like *khyo ga*."

The arrangement had Tenzin and Migmar's complete approval. They took seriously the task of seeing their four off-spring well married. Only one child remained unattached: Lhadon. Since her teenage years, Lhadon had learned to grace-fully straddle middle-class American and Tibetan American lifestyles. She seemed to live with their contradictory messages: be strong vs. be demure; be independent vs. be dependent on your father and brothers; step out and explore vs. integrate into your own community; share household responsibilities with brothers vs. do all the housework yourself or with other women.

After she graduated from high school, Lhadon had dated in casual coed groups with other young people of color—Hmong, Tibetan, and Cambodian. Dates, not even called dates, con-sisted of evening snacks or meals out, drinks, and dancing. I sensed parental unease with her adoption of such social prac-tices, harmless as they appeared to me. On the morning when Lhadon returned home from an all-night party in Milwaukee to celebrate her twenty-first birthday, I arrived by chance just in time to witness Migmar yelling and pounding on the bathroom door in a rare display of outrage.

Lhadon had locked herself inside. I didn't need a translator to understand how angry he was.

Lhadon moved out of her parents' home and rented a studio apartment for a year. She worked in a senior care facility and had her own income. She purchased fashionable clothes, a laptop, and a cell phone. Always generous, she bought a television and sofa set for her parents, clothes for her brothers, and giant-sized toys for her small niece and nephew.

When Tenzin found out that Lhadon's latest boyfriend gam-bled, she seemed to rev into high velocity, consulting friends and family from Madison to India. It was time to get serious about finding a proper fiancé for her daughter. Proper, of course, meant Tibetan. He could be Tibetan American, Tibetan Indian, even Tibetan Swiss, but he had to be Tibetan.

Lhadon's friend Wangmo lived around the corner and Wangmo mentioned to Lhadon that she had a handsome cousin in Nepal named Tenzin Dechen. She mentioned the idea to her mother, Sangmo, as well, and soon the two mothers, Sangmo and Tenzin, were actively promoting Wangmo's suggestion to Lhadon.

Lhadon and Dechen met via Skype and liked each other almost immediately. Dechen lived in the same Nepali-Tibetan community where Sangmo and her family had lived before they, like Tenzin's family, had come to Madison.

Seven months after they began talking online, a very excited Lhadon announced, "Dechen invited me to come to Nepal!" I raised my eyebrows. This seemed to me to be proceeding quickly, but for Tenzin, the idea that her daughter would venture unaccompanied to Nepal to meet a young man was unacceptable. She made a long-distance call to Dechen's mother in Nepal and introduced herself. The two mothers agreed their children seemed to be a good match and that it was high time they get married.

"We're all going to Nepal," Lhadon informed me a few days later. "I'm going to get married."

I was horrified.

She had never met this Tenzin Dechen person, much less considered the challenges that marriage, much less an international one, would involve. I fired off question after question, determined to help her realize she didn't know enough about him.

"How much schooling has he had? Does he read well? Does he speak English well? What does he want to do with his life? Who's in his family? What do you admire about him? What worries you about him? Have you talked to his parents? Has he talked with your parents?"

Lhadon stood her ground. Except for meeting his parents, she answered my questions with knowledge and confidence.

As a white, female, American divorcee, my advice—to first get to know him better—didn't fit Lhadon's or her parents' sense of urgency—an urgency that said a young woman should marry in her twenties and that the family's reputation depended on an honorable match.

I heard echoes of Tenzin's mother, Pema Choedon, pushing Tenzin toward marriage. No one had ever pushed me "toward," just pushed me to "wait," to "stay in," then "get out." I changed my approach. Might I, too, accompany them to Nepal for the wedding? Perhaps I could step in and protect Lhadon if it was obvious the marriage looked to be a grave mistake.

Though she brimmed with excitement at the time, Lhadon would confess to me a year later that she had also felt scared.

"After I learned my mother had talked to his mother, there was no going back," she said. "I felt stuck. I thought, 'Oh, well. I'll take a chance.' I figured if we didn't like one another at first, we could at least try to grow to love one another. If that didn't work, at least I could say to my parents, 'I married a Tibetan.' They're always telling me how good Tibetan men are as husbands."

Tenzin, Migmar, and Lhadon bought their plane tickets, Madison to Kathmandu, as did neighbor Sangmo and her husband. Lhadon's brothers and sisters-in-law would have loved to take time off from their jobs, but the combined fares would have been exorbitant. Tenzin sent money to India so that six relatives, including her sister Dickey and Dickey's two children could join us in Nepal for the ceremony. Acho Gawa and his wife, Ani Choenzom, came from Bylakuppe to represent Migmar's side of the family. In all, we'd be eleven Nepal-bound guests.

We were going to be there for more than a month. "At least marry him at the end of the month," I cautioned Lhadon. "That way, if you don't like him, you can come home." I tried to imagine myself at her age, flying together with my parents to a foreign country to marry a person I had never met. Were there truly no American or Tibetan American men for Lhadon in Wisconsin or in the whole United States? I saw a new, self-assured Lhadon emerging, a fascinating amalgam of the contemporary Western woman and a graceful, dutiful daughter, faithful to her parents' and culture's values.

"It's too late, Madeline," she responded consolingly. "They already consulted with the monks. The date is set, a lucky day. That's important. The wedding will be performed on the third day after we arrive."

My heart sank. Of course, the date needed to be auspicious, chosen after consultation with the ancient Tibetan calendar, built upon astrological tables, lunar cycles, and attention to the elements of earth, air, fire, and water. Plane tickets were already purchased, relatives invited, and money dispatched to set the marriage in motion. If this was to be such a propitious occasion, why did I feel sick to my stomach?

A month later, Lhadon and I sat together on the transatlantic flight, both nervous. In transit in Delhi, our paths separated. My ticket, purchased later, hadn't matched her family's itinerary exactly. I arrived in Nepal eight hours after Lhadon and her parents, disappointed not to be with them to meet the future husband.

Later Lhadon told me that in the chaos of Kathmandu's Tribhuvan International Airport, a smiling, confident man strolled toward her and hugged her as if they were old friends. She laughed in embarrassment. Migmar and Tenzin nodded shyly at Dechen, their soon-to-be son-in-law. Piles of luggage rotated around on a rumbling belt.

"It's missing!" Tenzin exclaimed to Migmar as the last of the bags came off the belt.

"What's missing?"

"The one with the jewelry!"

In Chicago, we had tried to board with a small carry-on containing Tenzin's heirloom jewelry for Lhadon to wear at the wedding, plus two beautiful traditional *chupa* dresses for Tenzin and me. The flight attendant tagged the bag and promised it would be waiting for us in Kathmandu. Somewhere between flights and continents, it disappeared.

When I arrived, only Lhadon and Dechen met my flight, beaming and holding hands. They informed me of the missing suitcase. Less worried about lost luggage than the compatibility of the bridal couple, I studied Dechen as he negotiated in Nepali with bored-looking officials. We left the airport without the missing suitcase. Lhadon would have to borrow necklaces, and Tenzin and I could borrow *chupas*. From the backseat of our taxi, with my backpack stacked atop the huge duffel bag that Tenzin had delegated to me to carry to Nepal, I apprehensively scrutinized the couple who were crammed next to the driver. Dechen placed his arm possessively around Lhadon's shoulders, and she snuggled against him.

They got out at Dechen's brother's apartment for their first night together. I hugged her and whispered, "Don't get pregnant." As the taxi pulled away, I chided myself on not having chosen something more poetic to say, but the practical side of me worried about the inconvenience of an unintended pregnancy at this time in their new relationship. After the wedding, they would be separated again while awaiting a spousal visa for Dechen.

The taxi dropped me off at a funky hotel, where Dechen's brother, who worked as the hotel receptionist, had secured us its best rooms at discounted rates. Tenzin, Migmar, and the five relatives from India awaited me in our third-story room, which looked out on Bodhnath Stupa, the largest stupa in Nepal, just across the street. A stupa marks a sacred spot where ashes of a holy person, often Buddha himself, were interred. Bodhnath Stupa is revered by Tibetans in exile for its ancient history and its accessibility, since they can no longer visit sites in old Tibet, should they even still exist.

I stared out the window. Bodhnath Stupa was a fat, imposing, white building with two large, serious eyes painted on each side of the pinnacle. The eyes seemed to stare at me and the bustling shoppers on the streets below, hurrying home as darkness fell. Suddenly the hotel room lights blinked, and a blackout zigzagged across the city, erasing the stupa from my sight. Migmar found a candle stub, and the eight of us gripped the banister to parade downstairs in single file to find the kitchen. Tenzin held the candle while Dickey and Ani Choenzom groped about cupboards for pots, then cut vegetables and boiled rice. The stub flickered over the torn plastic table cloth. Relieved travelers, happy to be united after our long trip, we enjoyed our first dinner together. On the streets outside, the crowds of people continued homeward, seemingly used to Kathmandu's routine blackouts.

Our arrival coincided with Buddhist Nepal's fifteen-day New Year celebration, Losar. Losar's opening ceremonies had concluded, but while we traveled about Nepal for the wedding and pilgrimage afterward, the crowds at Bodhnath grew daily. As Migmar breathed in the intense religious activity everywhere about us, at home in his familiar language and culture, respected as father of the bride, I realized I had seen only one small part of him.

The blackout continued into early dawn of the next day, as we set out to do a *kora*, our daily walk around a chosen temple. This morning it was to be Bodhnath. Linking arms, we dashed

across the heavily trafficked street in brave pairs, dodging honking cars. With hundreds of other pilgrims, we thronged past the
metal gates onto the stupa grounds. We began to circumnavi-
gate Bodhnath, our figures a blur in the dim light. Women, both
old and young, wore long-skirted *chupas*, with shawls or nylon
jackets for warmth, while older men walked hatless, in black
leather jackets. The pedestrian traffic traveled clockwise at a
brisk pace. Flickering candles lined our path, and pigeons
swooped like bats to eat grains that elderly ladies sprinkled on
the cement walkways. Thousands of prayer flags, suspended
from the central spire to the ground, whipped in the wind,
sounding like a herd of yaks in stampede.

"*Om Mani Peme Hung,*" elders prayed aloud, spinning the
hundreds of prayer wheels at the base of the stupa. The Tibetan
pronunciation of the ancient Sanskrit prayer, the jewel lotus
mantra, reverberated in the air. Tibetan Buddhists believe the
six spoken syllables of that phrase link the devout to the path of
enlightenment. Each syllable inspires ancient teachings of the
Lord Buddha into reminders of the six practices: the perfection
of generosity, pure ethics, tolerance and patience, perseverance,
concentration, and wisdom.

Returning from the stupa, we ate breakfast in our small
room, sitting on the edges of beds and cots. During our weeks
of travel together, we ate no restaurant meals. Dickey, Ani
Choenzom, and Acho Gawa took turns rising before sunrise
to fry breads and boil vegetables, always finishing in time to
do *kora*. Dickey's two high school–aged children slept in, waking only after we returned and immediately checking their
iPods to see what they were missing back home in Delhi.

After breakfast, Lhadon, Dechen, and Dechen's brother
joined us as we twelve crammed into a taxi van for the six-hour,
wedding-ceremony-bound drive to Dechen's settlement near
Pokhara, in the middle of Nepal. I had journeyed the same road

twenty-five years earlier, en route to a trekking adventure. Then, I had bounced atop a lumbering bus on a dirt road that wobbled toward pristine, terraced mountains. Now the paved, still bumpy highway was crowded with honking trucks, racing past garbage-lined rivers. The mighty Himalayan range lay somewhere behind a gray fog of pollution.

~

We arrived at Dechen's refugee settlement in the early afternoon. The term "refugee camp" elicits images of rows of tents and crowds of ragged children. But Nepal's refugee settlements for Tibetans have existed for more than fifty years, and tents have long since given way to cement-block structures built by inhabitants themselves. Dechen explained that Tibetans in Nepal would be more prosperous and integrated except that the government had acted inconsistently, previously granting and then withdrawing a path to citizenship. Without citizenship, exiled Tibetans could not own a home, land, or their own business. They remained trapped between the knowledge that they should have rights as citizens and conversely, their allegiance to the Tibetan ideal, that someday they will be citizens in a free Tibet.

The Jampaling Tibetan Settlement housed about three hundred families when I visited. What it lacked in prosperity was mitigated by its spectacular setting. One of the Himalaya's mightiest mountains, Annapurna, towered in the distance. As our van bumped down stony roads, I heard elders chanting prayers through the open windows of a nursing home. The smattering of buildings and the feeling of one country within another reminded me of Wisconsin's Native American communities.

As the driver unloaded our luggage, Dechen's friendly family members came running to embrace us warmly.

"*Chabi nan go! Chabi nan go!*" ("Welcome! Welcome!")

"*Tashi delek, tashi delek!*" we answered back.

Dechen's father and mother, grandparents, aunts and uncles, and four siblings all talked at once, crowding around the van. The youngest brother roared up on a motorcycle, helmet-less, his punk-style hair pointed straight heavenward. Our luggage disappeared somewhere.

"They are a good family," Tenzin had told me back in Madison. "Poor, but good. Poor—I have nothing against poor. I know poor. But good—that is what is important."

We found our bags set atop floor mattresses in a cement-block apartment. A schoolteacher had given up his home for us, just a few steps from Dechen's parents' home. Wedding preparations were in full steam beneath a tent awning.

"This will be the grandest wedding that ever occurred in Jampaling Tibetan Settlement. You won't have to lift a finger!" A woman beamed at me, revealing missing teeth. Thirty-six neighbors were enlisted as wedding cooks, servers, arrangers, and decorators. In the shade of a mango tree, Tenzin was handing over stack after stack of banded, faded rupee bills to Dechen's mother, the equivalent of about two thousand US dollars. Working three simultaneous minimum-wage US jobs made her a wealthy woman, by Nepali standards.

As the clouds around Annapurna turned pink, then bright red, we guests, with no assigned tasks, took a walk. "What jobs can young people get?" I asked Dechen, with an ear toward his future employment in the United States.

"There were no jobs here for me after I graduated from high school," he said. "My friends and I have to go to Pokhara or Kathmandu to find work. Busboy. Cook. Hotel reception. Driver." He recited the big-city possibilities. One brother was a monk, his sister worked at a Tibetan charity, while he and another brother clerked at the Kathmandu hotel where we had stayed.

Nepal remains one of Asia's poorest countries, where a family of four might survive on the equivalent of two hundred dollars a month. Refugee networks actually give Tibetan Nepalis a leg up compared to many of their countrymen. I wondered if Dechen realized that many young people his age in the United States had graduated from universities or technical schools, traveled widely, and already held leadership positions in volunteer organizations or at their job sites. Even without these advantages, though, Dechen would have the advice and encouragement of Lhadon's cohesive community, perhaps more support than many young Americans could claim.

∽

Though not allowed to lift a finger in the main house, Tenzin directed our wedding preparations in the borrowed apartment.

"Migmar-lak and Gawa-lak, stuff these envelopes!" Migmar and Acho Gawa filled blue envelopes with monetary gifts for family and helpers, carefully hand-lettering each envelope in rounded Tibetan script with the words *Tendrel Tsonje* (On an Auspicious Occasion). I handed Tenzin more bands of rupee bills, about four hundred dollars, to be given to our expanded family, pleased to be asked to cover my share.

Preparations continued into the dusk, and Annapurna dissolved into soft gray hues. As if on cue, a chorus of crickets burst into a rhythmic drone. Under the nimble fingers of neighbors, hundreds of Kleenex flowers bloomed on tables and were glued onto glittery, hand-printed "Happy Wedding" wall posters. The cooking tent became an aromatic bustle of order as women shouted, water ran, and pots banged. Compared to her brothers' wedding, Lhadon's felt closer to nature, with everything endearingly handmade. Tenzin whispered to me that no dancing or singing would be allowed, out of respect for the immolations of the previous three years. Although these wedding preparations were welcome and merry, the fiery deaths were not far from the thoughts of the guests. I rarely read anything about the immolations in the US media but now took notice of the long banners with hand-printed lists of names, hanging on temples we passed. Beside each name was the date of immolation and the person's age and home village or monastery. In respect for their sacrifice, all celebrations that year and the year before, including the New Year's holiday just past and this very wedding, were to be muted. Unlike most weddings, Lhadon's celebration would feature no performances by local artists and no dancing by guests long into the night.

As I sensed the souls of the monks hovering in the shadowy night, my disappointment at the absence of folk dance, which I loved, dissipated. Around the edges of inky clouds, bright stars appeared.

❧

I had only glimpsed Lhadon occasionally since arriving, as the bride is traditionally hidden from the guests. When she had stopped by our apartment so that her Aunt Dickey could practice the complex hair braiding for the wedding day, she looked assured and happy, so I tried to set aside my own worries. With the multiday wedding preparations well under way, it seemed too late for advice or delay tactics.

A soft sunrise marked the morning of the first wedding day. Before anyone stirred, an elder lama arrived from the local temple. Lhadon and Dechen sat alone before him at the family shrine, holding hands as he chanted for a full two hours. The rest of us rose, ate breakfast, and dressed for the blessing ceremonies to follow. The ritual prayers intoned wishes for the couple's happy life and set expectations for the bridal couple's respect for one another and for their elders. Afterward, Lhadon's back ached with the rigor of the straight posture expected of a bride.

After the lama had finished, both families crammed into the small living room of Dechen's parents, and the day became a continuous haze of white silk as guests bestowed *khata* on the couple. In addition to the traditional ceremonial scarves, the bride's family members, including me, greeted each of the seated groom's family with a blue envelope and a brightly wrapped gift box. The boxes contained Nike trainers or leather jackets for the men and brand-name purses for the women. We had lugged them in our duffel bags, probably returning made-in-Asia goods to Asia.

Except for the bride and groom, who remained stationary, the seating arrangement then switched. Now it was us, Lhadon's family, who sat on the linoleum floor atop fat pillows and nodded as each of Dechen's family members, whose names I could not remember, gave us blue envelopes. Mine contained 555 rupee bills, about seven dollars at home, but equivalent to a full day of someone's salary in Nepal. Lines of no fewer than three hundred friends and neighbors curled out the door, through the yards, and down the road, as guests began offering *khata* and their best wishes. They bowed first at the family's small shrine, with its portrait of the Dalai Lama, then to the parents and grandparents, and finally to the bride and groom. Envelopes piled before the newlyweds.

"Take that money and hide it!" Dechen's grandmother gestured vehemently now and then to a granddaughter. The pile was whisked away, only to grow again.

Dechen and Lhadon, wondrously clad in traditional silks and their furry Tibetan caps (*shamo gasse*), accepted *khata* and congratulations for hours. Lhadon's bridesmaid cousin removed piles of scarves from around their necks. By the end of the day, a white mountain of scarves shimmered near the shrine.

The proud head cook finally peeled himself away from the cauldrons to stand at attention before a lineup of sixteen aluminum tins piled with rolled *tigmo* breads, buffalo curry, fried chicken, Nepal's ubiquitous *dal bhat* (thin lentil soup), mushroom-spinach soup, and fancy puddings. Perceiving that I was an honored guest, a beaming serving woman pushed me to the serving table and gestured, "Eat! Eat!" I took my time, asking about various dishes, repeating pronunciations of the labeled ones. Almost through the long buffet, I glanced behind me. A retinue of lamas and monks followed. Behind them were both sets of parents of the bride and groom, then the bride and groom themselves.

I imagined I heard a whispered buzz and felt my cheeks flame as red as my blouse. But the meal line proceeded and others got up to join it, elders first, out-of-town guests next, followed by neighbors, and lastly children and helpers. I set my plate down, as if I had been merely collecting research samples. I photographed it and did not eat a bite.

It wasn't the first time I found myself the amused talk of the room, having missed a dozen cues clear to everyone else. Over the years, I'd developed a thin armor. I entertained friends with stories about times I had been in the wrong line, on the wrong train, in the wrong house, or atop the wrong mountain. On a trip to Japan, I had once carefully copied down what I thought to be the characters of the street name of my modest inn so that I could find it when I returned. Lost as usual, I showed the note to passersby. "Where is this?" I asked in my simple Japanese. They merely smiled and shook their heads; it turned out my lopsided characters spelled out, "One way, do not enter."

Still, my error in protocol, with its Ugly American overtone, presuming to be first in line and ignorant of local customs, smarted. But perhaps a coin of shame was a fair price to pay for the privilege of inclusion.

Even though dance and music were not allowed, the local temple had given Dechen's family dispensation to play cards and *bah*, a version of mah-jongg. Piles of crumpled bills accumulated on card tables as the afternoon gave way to spirited slapping and betting, mostly by men, but a few older women as well. Most of the women were busy with preparation of dinner, our second elaborate meal of the day, not with leftovers but with a completely new menu.

On day two, tables turned and the groom's family cooked for the helpers and neighbors, draped them in *khata*, and gave them each a blue envelope. Merriment spilled across the yards, as everyone except us stacked chairs and washed cauldrons. Lhadon worked alongside the groom's family.

"*Shok*, Lhadon!" they would call to her, beckoning her to come.

Still dressed in *chupa*, she blended with the graceful movements of the women as she joined their efforts to scrub pots and sweep floors. Lhadon smiled sweetly at her new mother-in-law and the elderly neighbors, who had their eyes constantly upon her, whispering among themselves. I hadn't realized I was going to lose someone at this wedding. She was one of them now, not just a part of Dechen's family, but a woman who had set girlhood aside. I missed my slightly wild, whimsical girl already.

After a few drinks that night, in the privacy of the living room, both fathers showed one another a few dance steps. Perhaps they had been talking about old dances seldom seen any more. Migmar was an accomplished singer and folk dancer, and the nickname of Dechen's father was *Gyalpo* (the King), after one of his well-remembered roles in Tibetan opera. The performance of Tibetan opera was forbidden in contemporary China, and in the years since Nepal's China-leaning government took power, permission for traditional opera performances in Nepal had been increasingly denied as well.

Tibetan opera was no less rich a folk arts tradition than Japan's highly esteemed *noh* or *kabuki* theater, which I had seen many times when I had lived there, and whose most famous actors were granted status as "Living National Treasures," recognized for their role in preserving invaluable arts. Without accompanying musicians, both fathers sang their parts, then hummed "dah dee di dum" where musicians were supposed to come in. Embarrassed by the old men's antics, younger family members made jokes during the dances. No one even bothered to lift a cell phone to take a video of these fragile remnants of a venerable art.

～

On the third day, *khata* again fluttered as the two families embraced. We lined up to say our good-byes. Women wiped their eyes.

"*Galaephe!*" "*Zhugpo chakpo nang go!*" Calls of "Go slow," like the English "take it easy," and "take care of your health" sent the travelers on their way

The Nepali family was losing a son, as Dechen fell in step with the Tibetan diaspora. Upon receiving his spousal visa, he would be putting oceans, politics, and the priorities of another country between himself and his aging parents. Maybe a sister or brother would visit him in the United States, but not his mother or father.

Our taxi van pulled away with sixteen people, including the bride and groom and guests to be dropped off here and there. A monastery's stack of borrowed cauldrons, pots, and pans rattled atop the roof. The taxi paused outside the settlement at the Seti River bridge. Dechen got out to tie a last *khata* scarf around the railing, to bless the home and health of those left behind. Against the paint-chipped metal supports, it whipped in the wind, one among dozens.

En route to a pilgrimage of Nepal's most famous Buddhist temples, our travel group added two of Dechen's brothers, including the monk, who knew Nepal's Buddhist history and had Buddhist friends at each temple. Acho Gawa and Ani Choenzom had looked forward to these days as the highlight of the trip. To my surprise, temple visiting was a busy, exhausting endeavor—we lit candles, drank holy water, inhaled incense, spun prayer wheels, touched holy stones, gave coins to beggars, left donations in wooden boxes, and asked the blessing of resident lamas. We wrote prayers on prayer flags and suspended them from the highest trees, sending our hopes skyward.

On the weathered wooden doors of each Tibetan Buddhist temple hung long, white sheets of paper or cloth, on which were inscribed the names and death dates of the monks and ordinary citizens who had self-immolated. As we journeyed from town to town, the lists grew longer and the dates of death more recent, often just the week before. The deaths felt very close, and voices seemed to whisper as willow and jacaranda trees swayed in the breezes.

Acho Gawa would pass away the following year, and Ani Choenzom the year after that. I had not even gotten around to sending them scrapbooks with photos of our shared journey. Beside me, breathing heavily, Ani Choenzom told me each day, as we climbed the steps to yet another temple, "Today is a dream of my lifetime."

Through our temple pilgrimage, Dechen and Lhadon teased one another and were gentle, gracious, and accommodating with us elders. I relaxed somewhat about the marriage. Dechen seemed solid and capable, as if he could climb mountains or weather storms. He was kind and open. I liked the way he looked gently at each new person he met, as if accepting that person directly into his heart. I liked the way all five siblings in his family shared cooking, playing cards, making jokes, and sleeping on sofas or carpets in one another's apartments. They glanced fondly at Lhadon, their new sister. Had I wasted all my worries? I bent my head and sighed with relief; it seemed I had.

Lhadon planned to remain another month, to get to know her new in-laws and husband better. She and Dechen talked non-stop about meeting on the US side, little aware that they would have to pass the toughest test of a spousal visa application— patience—as their papers would take not months, as they antic-ipated, but two years, to inch their way through US State Department bureaucracy.

~

Arriving back in Kathmandu at the end of the awe-inspiring temple circuit, we drove past the city's largest soccer field. Uni-formed Nepali soldiers marched in long lines, doing basic train-ing. "This used to be called Bhoe Thang [Tibet Ground]," Dechen informed us. "It's where the first Tibetan refugees who crossed the Himalayas on foot to Nepal stayed in 1959. They slept on the bare ground, under the stars, before UN tents arrived."

We drove on with our hired driver, those years far in the past, little suspecting that Nepalis would again be sleeping on the same bare ground, under cold, mean stars, following a mas-sive earthquake that would strike a few months later. Like Tibetans decades before, they would lie disoriented and anx-ious, wondering what the future held.

Just in time for the magnificent, early-morning finale on the fifteenth and last day of Losar, called Chonga Choepa, we jammed through the gates of Bodhnath Stupa. Long lines of chanting monks moved so slowly that we overtook them sev-eral times on our circular *kora*. Giant flames leapt from thick incense bundles they waved before them, purifying the path for the likeness of the Dalai Lama, whose gigantic, gold-framed portrait they carried.

The drone of their prayers, each voice soft, collectively filled the immense courtyard with a roar of piety. I lost count of our spellbound circles. Ritual fires burned on the stones outside the stupa. Flames of tiny candles jumped nervously back and forth in the wind, as if dubious about our prayers for peace. The chanting subsided. The monks crowded into the stupa interior. The new year was set upon its path, fervently blessed.

~

"It's here! They found it!"

Tenzin came running toward me as I passed through the casual security at Kathmandu Airport. Airport officials, recognizing us, approached victoriously, holding aloft the missing suitcase. The heirloom jewels were intact, as were the two wedding dresses. Had we been in the United States, an identifying bar code might have indicated where the missing suitcase had wandered. In Kathmandu, it kept its mystery to itself. At this point, it didn't seem to matter that the wedding had passed. The family's treasures had been restored, as had the honor of the uniformed employees. One nodded as we passed to our gate, eyebrows raised. "See? Not to worry."

~

As for my changing opinions about arranged, or almost-arranged, marriages, I queried my stepmother on my next Oklahoma visit. "Mom, could you have picked better spouses for us kids than we did for ourselves?"

She snorted as she glanced at family photos on the mantle, groupings that included former spouses who no longer attended reunions or graduations.

"I certainly could have!"

With help from those who knew me best, maybe I too would

still be married. Maybe I wouldn't have had to go around the world searching for families to "adopt."

Then again, maybe I would never have gotten to explore refugee settlements in India or temples in Nepal. Maybe I would know nothing about a small country called Tibet.

CHAPTER 15

◞

The Family Next Door

Love and compassion are necessities, not luxuries. Without them, humanity cannot survive.

—THE DALAI LAMA

All four children were launched. I had gone from being guide to a family with children to being a friend of a family of married, independent adults. Like any parent experiencing the empty nest, I felt nostalgia for our early days of innocence and my greater role in their lives.

Tenzin and Migmar continued to work cleaning Kennedy Manor apartment building, even as Migmar passed retirement age, their friendly smiles and steady presence as much a fixture as the shiny Otis elevators. The pair were punctual, always respectful, often cheerful, quick to laugh and to shrug off small slights. Others might have seen their work as menial, but I imagined Tenzin and Migmar could hear the words of the Dalai Lama echoing in the halls they swept: "I find hope in the darkest of days, and focus in the brightest. I do not judge the universe." Each push of the vacuum cleaner was an expression of love for their children and grandchildren, the next generations who would stand tall on their shoulders.

But even pillars of work ethic can start to crumble. "Let him retire," I repeatedly urged Tenzin, concerned about Migmar's health.

"A couple more years," she replied, before eventually coming around. "He can have the afternoons off, just work with me in the mornings."

In partial retirement, Migmar seemed delighted to fix lunch, babysit for his two grandchildren, and create mini-gardens of tomatoes and dahlias. Tenzin continued her night cleaning shift, 5 p.m. to 1 a.m.

Even as he took joy in the new generation, Migmar nursed fragments of memories from his old world. He had long ago lost track of his sister, Migkyi, whom he had last seen in Tibet the day his family escaped through a snowstorm. Year after year, he had wondered if she was still alive. He estimated she would be in her sixties.

Even though the Chinese Embassy invariably turned down Tibetan Americans' visa applications to travel to the Tibetan Autonomous Region, people had certain ways to inquire about relatives who had been left behind. This was especially true as increasing numbers of Western tourists began flocking to the region, and guides and tours flourished. Migmar wrote the name of his long-lost sister on a scrap of paper, and in less than a year's time, it passed from Lhakpa's relatives in Dharamsala to guides going to the TAR, and from there to people who actually knew the village, and finally to the family still living there. I imagined the scrap of paper, folded and refolded, smudged from handling, making this journey through many connected hands.

Miraculously, by a similarly circuitous route, word came back.

Migkyi was alive!

On the paper was her cell phone number, and soon they were able to talk by telephone. His old dialect and her modern

Tibetan, ever-changing as languages do in their home settings, made it difficult, but not impossible, to communicate. Everyone in both families sat excitedly beside these two siblings as they yelled into their phones, as if their voices must carry over the mountains and oceans separating them. Following the roundabout way their initial messages had arrived, Migmar sent money to Migkyi's family. Her grandchildren sent photos as simple cell phone attachments. Migkyi had raised four sons, all married with children of their own.

Heart soaring, Migmar applied to the Chinese Consulate in Chicago for a visa. Exceptions were being made occasionally, especially for Tibetan American elders with siblings and family still alive in China, but it was a long process without no guarantee of positive results.

Nine months later, a consulate employee called Migmar to schedule an interview to complete the visa application. Elated, Migmar planned to call Migkyi to tell her the good news. Instead, it was her son who called Migmar. His nephew told him Migkyi had passed away a month previously. The siblings had both lived long and full lives on separate continents—but their reunion, just a matter of months and some papers away, would never occur.

Migmar continued taking out the trash and mopping floors, but a tiny ember, protected so long, had been extinguished. He said prayers for Migkyi at a private blessing at Deer Park Temple and lit candles at his home shrine. He was now the last surviving member of his immediate family who had fled Tibet. He told the consulate to give his interview spot to someone else.

The Dalai Lama said, "Judge your success by what you had to give up in order to get it." By that measure, my old friend was one of the most successful people I knew.

～

As another layer of grief settled into Migmar's flesh, I nonetheless smiled to see Migmar laughing often that year, him in the center of his growing family, me as a frequent visitor. All four of Migmar and Tenzin's kids were in their twenties and thirties, creating families, homes, and careers. Newlyweds Lhadon and Dechen still lived in the roomy house on Midvale Avenue, poised to become Migmar and Tenzin's caretakers once they became older. Recently arrived to the United States via his spousal visa, Dechen was feeling his way around Madison's low-wage circuit, while Lhadon consistently piled on extra shifts at her nursing care jobs. At home, both seemed content to share the household tasks of shopping, cooking, and running errands with Tenzin and Migmar. Their devotion to the older couple engendered both approbation and shame in me, since I lived far from my stepmother and visited rarely.

Tamdin and his girlfriend circulated within Chicago's Tibetan American communities, Tseten a nurse and Tamdin headed for graduate school in physical therapy. On any major holiday or upon the occasion of each one of the Dalai Lama's visits to Madison, I encountered them in Migmar and Tenzin's living room, drinking tea, Tamdin regaling all with his adventures as a part-time urban cabbie, a job he held while he attended night classes and saved for tuition. He chortled about a celebrity baseball player who had missed his bus to Wrigley Field, and a shady passenger who refused to give any address. "Just drive. I'll tell you when to stop." Gay men wrote their phone numbers on the backsides of fare receipts and thrust the slips back to Tamdin.

The lives of the other two brothers were solid and suburban. Namgyal and Thardoe worked their maintenance and sales jobs, and their articulate wives, with grace and fearlessness, continued making Madison a better place to live.

"I prefer Madison's west side," Namgyal told me on one

cross-city drive, pointing out the homes of other Tibetan Americans who, like him, had small children and had moved into his same neighborhood. Lhakpa's sister and brother-in-law resided temporarily with them, using the guest bedroom, on an extended visit from India, hoping to claim asylum for US citizenship. Bedrooms in all their houses were put to good use as siblings, aging parents, monks, friends, and friends of friends needed places to stay when they passed through Madison en route to study at Deer Park Buddhist Center or to see the Midwest or to help care for newborns. They were part of an increasingly layered diaspora web—one whose tenuous connections became ever stronger and more solidly woven.

⁓

While I was one strand of that web, I had only limited success when I tried to connect Tenzin's family into the lives of my friends and my own nuclear family.

In different combinations over the years, one or three or all four of the kids had accompanied me on trips to visit my family in Oklahoma, Colorado, Nevada, and New York, and on canoe and camping outings in Wisconsin. Over time, my younger brother Will's family in Oklahoma, and certainly my sister Susan, met every single one—Migmar and Tenzin and all four kids. I invited various Madison friends to the family's Midvale Boulevard home to enjoy spicy dinners and play the ancient Indian board game Carram. I wanted others to fall in love with them, to experience their culture and their charm, and to begin inviting them to special events as I did. But my friends and family continued to view Tenzin and her family as "Madeline's friends."

They seemed slow to realize the new citizens in Madison were not mere appendages of my life. As friends and family continued to treat me as a single woman in spite of my large family, I sympathized with same-sex couples whose families are slow to acknowledge their partners as vital to their lives. Perhaps it was me who was to blame. At some point, as their own social lives filled with partners and parties, I ceased bringing Tenzin and her kids on my wide-ranging travels, then missed them when they weren't there.

Despite my integration attempts, certain facets of my life and of Tenzin's family's life remained stubbornly separate. Perhaps it was the language barrier; perhaps it was because I didn't fully embrace Tibetan Buddhism, since that religion, at least the culture around that religion, was central to their existence. Aspects of their religion fascinated and inspired me, but I made few attempts to study it seriously. My Oklahoma family's Unitarian Universalism—creedless, activist, thoughtful, even cerebral—had helped me embrace global studies, human rights, and immigrant justice. I carried these values with me on my travels as I entered ancient stone cathedrals, magnificent mosques, and ornate temples, always fascinated by the history, architecture, and rites practiced within, but never drawn toward conversion or conviction.

I felt a great humility when visiting these sacred places, a humility that echoed when I heard the Dalai Lama speak. This was a man who could have led his people to war. He could have used his words and influence to create a rhetoric of reclamation and righteousness. Yet he had done something more formidable: he had advocated compromise, compassion, patience, and forgiveness. He had formulated peace plans and had proposed a magnificent compromise with the government of the world's most populous nation. It was good to hear a man who lived simply, with both feet on the ground, yet talked about world peace and a freer Tibet as achievable goals. He walked a path that made both seem possible.

Perhaps because I involved myself in so many other aspects of Tibetan culture, many of my Madison acquaintances asked if I attended Buddhist services at Deer Park Temple or intended to join one of the city's *sangha* meditation communities. I myself awaited some epiphany of mindfulness, as if it were an assured result of rubbing elbows with Tibetan Buddhists.

My adopted family's religion was something personal to them, however; they never tried to impose it upon me. Only once, after my brother David died of a brain tumor, did they gently guide me to Deer Park Temple for a service they had requested for David's soul. Even then, it was as if the service was as much for their grief as mine; a death of an important person could not be left unacknowledged.

I had attended a family memorial for David in Portland but hadn't thought to include my Tibetan American family, even though they had spent time with him. During their Thanksgiving holiday with David in Oregon, David had introduced Tamdin, Thardoe, and Lhadon, then teenagers, to their first ocean. David, Susan, and I, three adults with no children of our own, had laughed to see them jumping, shouting, and turning cartwheels on the cold autumn sands of Canon Beach. It had been a glorious, stolen moment with someone else's children, witnessing their exultance at encountering the ocean's raw power and majesty. The moment sparkled as an unexpected jewel on the chain that did in fact connect my two families.

"We would have sent someone to your brother's memorial," Tenzin said in a soft voice, perhaps the closest she had ever come to chiding me.

∽

Rather than looking for more connections, I decided perhaps it was time to begin loosening ties. Well established in their US homes, Tenzin's family no longer seemed to need their American guide. Where did I fit in? Should I redirect my efforts elsewhere—perhaps see if a more recent refugee family could use a hand? I needed to be needed, to feel essential, to be the protagonist in my own narrative. I desired to be connected, to love and be loved. Was the old loneliness creeping in? We would always be close, but it seemed time to pull back on my involvement, to let go with hope and affection. We all needed to make room for what was next in our individual and collective stories.

Though I felt blue about the change, the pause for reflection reminded me to take stock of the many gifts this family had given me over the past decade and a half. At the top of this list of blessings were the love on both sides and my gratitude for the place I held in the family, as honorary auntie and mentor. I had experienced the mystery and frustration with teens as they grew into adulthood. I had dampened tissues with tears at their high school graduations, citizenship ceremonies, and weddings. My holidays had taken on new hues and aromas. My trips to India, China, and Nepal and the invitations to stay in homes and monasteries of Tibet's far-flung diaspora were duplicated on no tourist itinerary. These weren't foreign countries to me anymore, but homes to my extended family—Dickey and her kids in Delhi, Dechen's siblings near Pokhara. Beyond our shared memories and traded traditions, I had attained an education found on no college campus. I had caught the family in a moment of fast, fascinating transition and witnessed America's immigrant story from a front-row seat. I had seen faraway global issues, such as human rights abuse and cultural genocide, move from impersonal to personal, from Tibetan jails to marches in Madison, from children walking across mountains on one continent to children studying in Saturday schools on another.

Migmar kept reminding me, by his actions, not his words, that each day had gifts, but I had to be open to them. Pouring water into the offering cups, he focused on its clarity, the low octave of liquid on liquid, the dance of sunlight on the silver. Through his patience with and acceptance of the small beauties of each day, he

taught me to sense layers of deeper meaning. Tenzin taught me
how generosity ripples outward, multiplying kindness. She
showed me how we may find true family in unexpected places.

The family's overarching gift to me, however, was that they
practiced peace as something achievable, something that communities of people tackle in small, daily tasks. Before peace is
a reality, it must exist as a dream and a vision, its story nurtured,
repeatedly told and changed in the retelling.

A lifelong pacifist, I have collected anecdotes about how
people achieve peace, whether within themselves or in their
communities. Peace is a fine thing to advocate, another to practice, a lesson that activists repeatedly try, fail, and relearn. Still,
the years with Tenzin's family empowered me to see how many
doors open when one simply says hello to the family next door.
Walking through that door, I found rooms of religion, ethnicity,
and class painted in unexpected iridescence, colors that altered
my world view forever.

Inspired by Tenzin, Migmar, and their family, I approached
my Peace Corps years in dry, dusty Lesotho, Africa, with a new
openness, aware, even from the first day there, of how my life
was already connected to people I had not yet met. I felt ready
to learn what they had to teach. I knew, somewhere in mountain
villages with thatch-roof huts, that families awaited me, no matter how fragmented they might seem—some without parents,
perhaps just a grandmother or neighbor caring for orphaned
children. Beyond Lesotho there would later be other families,
of other configurations, each different from the one preceding,
all needing peaceful environs in which to flourish. Our shared
future, the barometer of global strength and humanity, depends
on whether these families will be nurtured by compassion, care,
and empathy. All families have something to teach one another.
If global issues such as violence, pollution, and overpopulation
exist, in microcosm, at the family level, so too do the solutions.

The gifts we give one another can ease suffering, engender hope, and even shorten wars.

⌒

My idealism survived Lesotho's tough tests of poverty. When I returned from my Peace Corps service in 2012, I was delighted to reconnect with Tenzin's family and thrilled to meet its newest addition, energetic Choesang, who was Namgyal and Lhakpa's two-year-old daughter. I was dismayed, however, to find everyone in the family—parents and grandparents, aunts and uncles—speaking to her in often broken, always accented English.

"Oh, my gosh! Don't speak English to her!" I told them, resuming my know-it-all role. "You must speak Tibetan to her. Don't worry, she'll learn English just fine."

Migmar and Tenzin seemed relieved as I tried to summarize the recommendations of dual-language acquisition research. Day after day, Choesang stood on her tiptoes, her nose pressed right up against the big-screen TV, to watch *Sesame Street* and Disney videos. She was immediately able to sing and dance and chant in English, her only accent that of the midwestern American cornfields.

"Please, Migmar, tell her those wonderful old tales in Tibetan," I begged, remembering how much his children had loved their father's stories. Choesang listened with rapt attention. She had a special relationship with her Emi, her paternal grandfather.

Fascinated, I watched Choesang's language transition: first speaking only Tibetan, then very quickly after that becoming bilingual in Tibetan and English, and finally, mostly communicating in English. When her parents spoke to her in Tibetan, she answered in English. But to her grandfather Migmar, she consistently spoke Tibetan.

She proudly sang the Alphabet Song and counted to one hundred in perfect English, the center of everyone's attention, dancing around on the living room carpet. We applauded, then asked her to recite the Tibetan alphabet.

"Ka, kah, ga, nga; ca, cha, ja, nya," she began, less confidently. She finished and we beamed and applauded again, none more enthusiastically than Migmar. Unlike the twenty-six letters on *Sesame Street*, however, Choesang did not hear the thirty Tibetan letters often. I saw how almost everything in her world reinforced English. I was sorry I couldn't help her. The Tibetan language was familiar to me—I could recognize it on the street—but despite my many years with the family, I had only picked up an occasional phrase. I wanted to fill Choesang's bedroom with picture books and games and DVDs in the language of her grandfather, but the few books I could find seemed old-fashioned, and I did not find any children's cartoons or movies in Tibetan.

But as I heard Lhakpa continue to speak to her daughter in Tibetan, and sing to her Tibetan songs such as "Sun Da Lemo So," I knew she was headed down a well-trodden path. Soon Choesang would go to Saturday school, filled with friends her age and a lively dance group, where she would learn about her heritage and become one of the next generation to keep blowing on precious embers of Tibetan culture. Innocent now, she would soon be strong enough to understand the tough lessons in the Tibetan curriculum. She would tell her own story, perhaps even retell her grandparents' stories, in her own clear voice. She would grow up spanning two worlds, as this family's first American-born child, nurtured by people on two continents who cherished her.

And I was honored to be one of them.

Tibetan Name Meanings

Tibetan names are profound and meaningful, often with religious and spiritual significance. Because it is sometimes difficult to translate precisely into other languages, the below meanings are simplified and approximate. I have also provided pronunciations as an English speaker would say them. R is a soft r; oe is similar to German umlaut ö; ts sounds almost like s, as in the word tsunami.

Choedon (CHÖ-dohn)	One who is devout or religious
Choenzom (CHÖN-zohm)	Plentiful dharma (Buddhist spirituality)
Choesang (CHÖ-sahn)	Excels at practice of the dharma (Buddhist spirituality); noble qualities
Damdul (DAHM-dool)	Conquerer of evils, enemies
Dawa (DAH-wah)	Monday or moon
Dechen (DEH-chen)	Great bliss
Dickey (DICK-ee)	Healthy and wealthy, or healthy and happy
Dolma (DOHL-mah)	One who liberates others from suffering
Dorjee (DOR-jeh)	Indestructible diamond
Gawa (GAH-wah)	Joyful
Gyalpo (GYAL-poh)	King
Gyatso (GYAT-soh)	Ocean of enlightened qualities

Jampa (JAHM-pah)	Loving kindness
Jamyang (JAHM-yahng)	Gentle voice
Jangchub (JANG-chub)	Enlightenment, awakened state
Kalsang (KELL-sahng)	Good fortune
Karma (KAR-mah)	Action, deed
Kunsel (KOON-sell)	Total clarity
Lhadon (LAH-dohn)	Goddess of adornment
Lhakpa (LHAK-pah)	Wednesday or the planet Mercury
Lhamo (LAH-moh)	Goddess
Migkyi (MINK-kee)	Joyful Tuesday
Migmar (MIG-mahr)	Tuesday or the Planet Mars
Namdol (NAHM-dohl)	Complete victory or liberation
Namgyal (NAM-gyahl)	Victorious
Nawang (NAH-wahng)	Powerful speech
Norbu (NOR-boo)	Jewel
Norzom (NOR-zuhm)	Abounding in wealth
Paldon (PAHL-dohn)	Glorious
Pema (PEH-mah)	Lotus
Sangmo (SAHNG-moh)	Good-hearted woman
Sopa (SOH-pah)	Patience
Tamdin (TAHM-deen)	A name to expel bad spirits
Tenpa (TEN-pah)	Teaching of the dharma (Buddhist spirituality)
Tenzin (TEN-zeen)	Holder of the teachings or protector of the dharma (Buddhist spirituality)
Thardoe (THAR-dö)	Wishes to be liberated
Tsamchoe (TSAHM-chö)	Cutting off evil spirits
Tsedup (TSE-duhp)	Longevity

Tseten (TSEH-ten)	Stable life
Tsering (TSEHR-ring)	Long life
Wangdu (WAHNG-doo)	Conqueror
Woeser (WÖ-ser)	Sunlight or radiance

Suggested Readings

If you wish to learn more about Tibetan culture and the experiences of refugees, here are some books I particularly enjoyed.

For Adults

Brauen, Yangzom. *Across Many Mountains: A Tibetan Family's Epic Journey from Oppression to Freedom.* New York: St. Martin's Press, 2011.

Dalai Lama XIV. *Freedom in Exile: The Autobiography of the Dalai Lama.* San Francisco: Harper, 1991.

Das, Lama Surya. *Awakening the Buddha Within: Tibetan Wisdom for the Western World.* New York: Broadway Books, 1998.

Dorjee, Tenzin. *The Tibetan Nonviolent Struggle: A Strategic and Historical Analysis.* Washington, DC: ICNC Press, 2015.

Dolma, Kunsun, with Evan Denno. *A Hundred Thousand White Stones: An Ordinary Tibetan's Extraordinary Journey.* Sommerville, MA: Wisdom Publications, 2013.

Faderman, Lillian, with Ghia Xiong. *I Begin My Life All Over: The Hmong and the American Immigrant Experience.* Boston: Beacon Press, 1998.

Hanh, Thich Nhat. *The Heart of the Buddha's Teaching: Transforming Suffering into Peace, Joy, and Liberation.* New York: Broadway Books, 1999.

Sambhaya, Padma, ed. *The Tibetan Book of the Dead: The Great Book of Natural Liberation Through Understanding in the Between.* New York: Bantam Books, 1993.

Sopa, Geshe Lhundub, with Paul Donnelly. *Like a Waking Dream: The Autobiography of Geshe Lhundub Sopa.* Sommerville, MA: Wisdom Publications, 2012.

Yang, Kao Kalia. *The Latehomecomer: A Hmong Family Memoir.* Minneapolis: Coffee House Press, 2008.

For Young Readers

Berger, Barbara. *All the Way to Lhasa: A Tale from Tibet.* New York: Philomel Books (Penguin), 2002. (Ages 4–8)

Dolphin, Lourie. *Our Journey from Tibet.* New York: Dutton Children's Books, 1997. (Ages 8 and older)

Gerstein, Mordicai. *The Mountains of Tibet*. Cambridge, MA: Barefoot Books, 2013. (Ages 5–8)

Gray, Nick with Laura Scandiffio. *Escape from Tibet: A True Story*. Toronto: Annick Press, 2014. (Ages 12–14)

Sis, Peter. *Tibet Through the Red Box*. New York: Farrar, Straus and Giroux imprint Frances Foster Books, 1998. Caldecott Honor Book. (Ages 11 and older)

Acknowledgments

I thought this would be a quick year's nonfiction endeavor. It took an additional three years, four writing groups, and several writing courses to realize the story was mine, not theirs, memoir, not exposition, and to pound my flowery prose into succinct sentences. Madison nurtures its writers! I am grateful to my writing groups for their feedback and their patience with my repeated submissions: Julie Tallard Johnson's kindly Writing Circle (Michael Brandmeier, Anne Liesendahl, Cameron Mac-Donald, Colleen Sims, Linda Sonntag, and Therese Unumb); the dogged Save the Lakes (Thomas Christopher, Tina Hartlaub, Marilyn Gardner, Jessica Gunderson, Star Oldermas, Judy Pasch, Ingrid Rothe, Tony Van Witsen, and Jody Whelden); the high-aiming Back Porch Writers (Chris Chambers, M. J. Kieffer Morishita, Deb Smith, Mary Tilton, Steve Verburg, and Evelyn Lasky-Westbrook); and the brave no-name femmes (M. J., Sonia Baku, and Catherine Erhard Olson). The outstanding Madison Writers' Studio (Susanna Daniels and Michelle Wildgen) and University of Wisconsin's comprehensive Department of Continuing Studies (Laurie Scheer, Angela Rydell, and Chris Chambers) provided me solid footing with online courses, evening seminars, and four consecutive Writer's Institutes, attended by hundreds of regional authors. "Sherpa" Julie Tallard Johnson read every word of the original manuscript and guided me along rocky paths, dotted with retreats at her country home, a virtual writing group at dawn, and insights from her inspiring weekly blog, *All Write Wednesdays*.

For assistance with various chapters, I leaned on the expertise of folklorist Richard March, educators Judith Garcia Landsman,

Amy Christianson, and Pam Delfosse, travelers Lewis Koch and Rachel Weiss, refugee advocates Kathleen Krchnavek and Savitri Tsering, and bloggers Jolma Ren (*Jolma's Kitchen*) and Lobsang Wangdu and Yolanda O'Bannon (*YoWangdu Tibetan Culture*). Finer points of Tibetan culture were illuminated by University of Wisconsin Tibetan instructor Genlak Jampa Khedup, as well as Genlak Kalsang Gyatso Kunor, Tenzin Tsamchoe-lak, and Patrick Lambelet. Friends Jon Ingham, Ed Wohl, Jan Christmas, Peter Williams, and Cynthia Sampson lent a pen or camera when needed, and Phil Martin of Crickhollow Books kept pointing the direction.

I have been an admirer from afar of the Wisconsin Historical Society Press. In closer range, I am awed by the calm professionalism of editor in chief Kate Thompson, editors Carrie Kilman and Erika Wittekind, marketing director Kristin Gilpatrick, and managing editor Diane Drexler.

I come from a family of storytellers, so I share creative DNA with dear siblings Susan, Will, and Kate, whose love sustains me. Most of all, special thanks to Tenzin Kalsang-lak and Migmar Dorjee-lak, and to their large and growing family—Namgyal Tsedup and Lhakpa Dolma, Nawang Lhadon and Tenzin Dechen, Tenzin Tamdin and Tseten Langchun, and Tenzin Thardoe and Tenzin Samkyi—for their willingness to share their story, for their patience with my naiveté, and most of all, for their years of friendship. To all, *thuk je che*—thank you!

About the Author

Madeline Uraneck is an educator and writer who has visited sixty-four countries through her work for the state of Wisconsin, several Peace Corps assignments, and her passion for world travel. As International Education Consultant for the Wisconsin Department of Public Instruction, Uraneck initiated programs to open the doors of hundreds of Wisconsin's K-12 classrooms to visiting language and culture teachers from Japan, Germany, Sweden, Thailand, Mexico, and China. As liaison to the International Education Council, a project of Wisconsin's governor and state education superintendent, she organized international education summits, global studies conferences, teacher workshops, and sister school and sister state exchanges.

In 2006, Uraneck arrived in Lesotho, southern Africa, as the oldest Peace Corps volunteer in her cohort, and went on to serve on the Peace Corps staff in Washington DC, Turkmenistan, and Kyrgyzstan. Her writing has appeared in K-12 curriculum materials, educational handbooks on culture and policy, and publications including *WorldView Magazine*, *Global Education*, *WorldWise Schools*, and *Isthmus*, where they won a 2007 Excellence in Wisconsin Journalism award from the Milwaukee Press Club.